THE COMPLETE GUIDE TO
TROPICAL AQUARIUM
FISH CARE

DAVID ALDERTON

ANIMAL CARE

THE COMPLETE GUIDE TO
TROPICAL AQUARIUM
FISH CARE

MITCHELL BEAZLEY

Executive Art Editor: Emma Boys
Executive Editor: Samantha Ward-Dutton
Produced for Mitchell Beazley by **PAGE**One
Cairn House, Elgiva Lane, Chesham, Buckinghamshire HP5 2JD
Production: Paul Hammond

First published in Great Britain in 1998 by Mitchell Beazley,
an imprint of Reed Consumer Books Limited
Michelin House, 81 Fulham Road, London SW3 6RB

ISBN 1-84000-037–6

A CIP catalogue of this book is available at the British Library.

Printed in Singapore

Contents

Introduction 6

What is a fish?

The evolution of fish 8

Breathing and buoyancy 10

Fish senses 12 • Osmosis 14

Body shape and fins 16

Sociability and aggression 18

Reproductive behaviour 20

Development of the fry 22

How the hobby developed 24

Group profiles

Factors to consider 26

Livebearers 28 • Cyprinids 30

Characins 32 • Anabantoids 34

Killifish 36 • Cichlids 38

Catfish 40 • Miscellaneous groups 42

Preparing an aquarium

Choosing an aquarium 44

The aquarium substrate 46

Plants 48 • Choosing the plants 50

Filtration equipment 52

Heaters and thermostats 54

Water conditions: pH 56

Water conditions: hard or soft? 58

Siting your aquarium 60

Setting up the aquarium 62

Planting and filling the tank 64

Hoods and lighting 66

Conditioning the water 68

Brackish water 70

Choosing and caring for fish

Buying fish 72 • Selecting your fish 74 • Settling in 76 • Catching fish 78 • Initial concerns 80 • Routine maintenance 82 • Breeding 84

Preparing for breeding 86

Rearing the fry 88

Feeding

Digestion and feeding habits 90 • Formulated foods 92 • Live foods 94

Health care

How illness spreads 96 Signs of illness 98 • Bacterial diseases 100

Fungal and viral diseases 102

Parasitic infections 104

Other parasitic problems 106

Coping in a crisis 108

Index 110

Acknowledgements 112

Introduction

Keeping tropical fish has grown into a huge hobby in little more than a century, thanks to the massive advances in technology which have brought electricity into homes, and led to the development of an ever-increasing array of aquarium equipment. Fish-keeping can provide an ideal antidote to a stressful lifestyle, and tropical fish may be kept without any problems even in high-rise apartments, where housing other pets such as dogs or cats would be impossible. As our lives become busier and our homes smaller, aquarium fish are a perfect way of keeping in touch with the natural world without being a tie. There are now even timed feeders to ensure the fish do not miss their regular meal if you do not come straight home from work!

Immense scope now exists in tropical fish-keeping and you can choose from a community aquarium, housing a variety of fish, through to specialist set-ups, accommodating collections such as African Rift Valley lake cichlids, annual killifish, or fish found in brackish water. The various options, and the fish themselves, are to be found within the following pages.

Choosing fish

This book profiles all the main groups of aquarium fish, as well as those which are commonly kept and yet cannot be fitted into a general category. Their basic characteristics, as well as their housing, feeding, and breeding requirements are discussed in some detail, enabling you to decide whether they are suitable for the type of set-up that you are planning, or, if you already have an aquarium, whether they can be added safely alongside the existing tank occupants. The key symbols in this part of the book also provide vital insight into the water conditions that the fish require – this alone may restrict your choice. The size of the fish is another important characteristic that needs to be considered at the outset. Young fish of all species are generally small, but some will grow much more rapidly than others and can represent a danger to their smaller companions. Compatibility is a vital consideration when setting up an aquarium of any type.

Preparing for the fish

Before acquiring the fish themselves, you will need to purchase an aquarium and other equipment. Having set up the aquarium, it is best to wait for a week or so to check that everything is functioning correctly and to allow the plants to become established, before adding the fish. Ordinary aquaria are relatively cheap, so it is a good idea to obtain a spacious unit, rather than having to replace a small tank as the fish start to grow.

It is vital to decide where to locate the tank at the outset before you start to assemble the various components and fill it. Once filled, an aquarium is likely to be too heavy to move, without having to be emptied again. A secure base is equally vital, to ensure that the weight of the aquarium is properly supported.

There is no need to worry if you feel that your technical skills may be inadequate when it comes to wiring up the heating, lighting, and filtration systems in the aquarium. Not only has technology in this area advanced rapidly over recent years, but it has also become increasing user-friendly, to the extent that stylish units of various sizes are available, which simply need to be filled up and connected to the power supply.

Caring for fish

You should only buy your fish from reputable suppliers, but on occasions, health problems may still arise within particular groups of fish. This is why it is always so important to check not just on the fish that catch your eye within a tank, but also on the others sharing their accommodation. Many ailments spread rapidly through the aquarium water, and, following the stress of a move to your home, even a healthy-looking fish may succumb if it has previously been exposed to infection. Only purchase fish from tanks where all the occupants appear to be healthy.

Breeding fish

While some fish will breed readily in a home aquarium, the requirements of others can be much more demanding, and represent a serious challenge for the experienced hobbyist. Detailed explanations of why this is the case, as well as information on the various breeding strategies used by fish, and how to rear their fry successfully can be found in the breeding section. Even if you have no previous experience of breeding fish, this book should set you on the path to success, enabling you to enjoy another facet of this fascinating hobby, including possibly the parental care shown by some groups of fish towards their young from the moment of spawning onwards. The development of and potential problems associated with the breeding of new colour and fin forms are also discussed.

Healthy living

The critical period in the health of the fish is likely to be the first couple of months in the new aquarium. During this time the filter bed is likely to be maturing as the fish settle in their new surroundings. The wide selection of specially formulated fish foods means that they should remain in top condition, provided that the water quality remains good. Regular partial water changes will be essential, and correct lighting will be equally necessary for lush plant growth in the aquarium.

Typical signs of illness are covered, enabling you to identify problems and react appropriately. This is not only important for the welfare of the sick fish itself, but can be equally significant for other occupants in the tank, which could otherwise be exposed to the serious threat of infection themselves. Remedies to treat fish ailments can be obtained from most aquatic stores, but they must be used strictly in accordance with the accompanying instructions if they are to afford the greatest likelihood of recovery.

Using this book

The aim of this book is to provide a sound basis for newcomers to fish-keeping, as well as providing further insight and guidance that will be of interest

Tropical fish-keeping is an increasingly popular hobby. Whatever the scale of your aquarium, the wide range of colourful species now avalaible will bring hours of pleasure.

to more experienced enthusiasts as well. I hope that the inclusion of topics relating to the basic biology of fish, which are often largely overlooked in most fish-keeping books, will give a better insight into the needs of this fascinating and diverse group of creatures. The aim has also been to incorporate the latest information on advances in the technological field, explaining how these can be of benefit to the fish themselves, as well as to those looking after them.

The book follows a natural progression, from introducing the characteristics of fish as a group and the development of tropical fish-keeping as a hobby through the various stages in setting up and maintaining an aquarium. Foodstuffs and feeding, breeding, and health care are also covered in individual sections. If you need to find specific pieces of information quickly therefore, you should be able to locate the required topics without difficulty, while overall, the book will provide an easily accessible and up-to-date guide to all aspects of looking after tropical fish successfully in the home.

What is a fish?

With their fluid movements and dazzling array of patterns, colours, and shapes, fish are a constant source of fascination. Today's extraordinary diversity of types stems from prehistoric ancestors, which were some of the earliest complex living creatures on Earth, making dinosaurs look like recent newcomers...

The evolution of fish

Fossils of fish remains date back over 500 million years, making them the oldest group of vertebrates (animals with backbones) on the planet. The earliest evidence of their existence comes from fossilized bony scales unearthed from rocks of the Cambrian period, but the first fish whose entire outline is known dates back to the subsequent Ordovician era.

Named *Arandapsis*, this fish is also the earliest known complete vertebrate. Just 15cm (6in) in length, it had a very simple body structure, with no fins, and depended entirely on its tail for propulsion. Its backbone or notochord was composed of stiff cartilage rather than bone. There are clear signs of gills for breathing in *Arandapsis*, but jaws – believed to have adapted from the first of the series of gill arches – had not yet developed at this stage in the evolutionary process.

Jaws!

Roughly 80 million years after the appearance of the earliest fish, jawed fish started to evolve. Jaws aided feeding and therefore survival, because fish no longer had to depend on tiny creatures and vegetable matter which they could swallow whole. There was a rapid increase in types of fish and much larger fish also began to develop, some of which became fearsome predators.

The most notorious of these are the sharks, whose lineage dates back over 400 million years, with remarkably few changes since then. But evolution did not stop there: fossils show that feeding techniques continued to develop over many millennia. For example, *Lepidotes* developed greater jaw mobility, enabling it to suck in prey directly, rather than having to seize it.

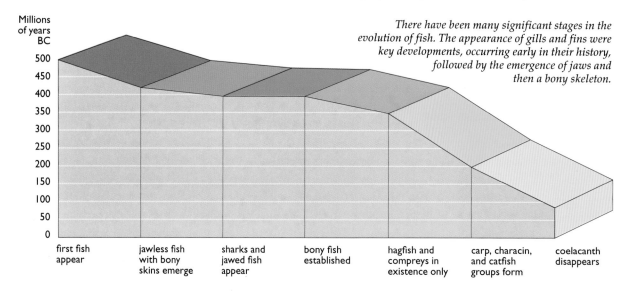

There have been many significant stages in the evolution of fish. The appearance of gills and fins were key developments, occurring early in their history, followed by the emergence of jaws and then a bony skeleton.

Millions of years BC

500
450
400
350
300
250
200
150
100
50
0

first fish appear | jawless fish with bony skins emerge | sharks and jawed fish appear | bony fish established | hagfish and compreys in existence only | carp, characin, and catfish groups form | coelacanth disappears

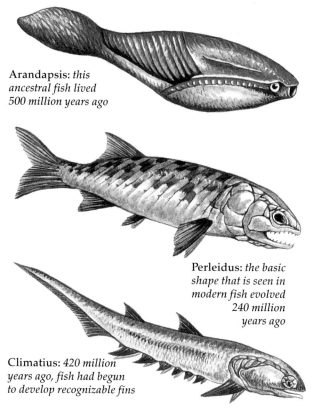

Arandapsis: *this ancestral fish lived 500 million years ago*

Perleidus: *the basic shape that is seen in modern fish evolved 240 million years ago*

Climatius: *420 million years ago, fish had begun to develop recognizable fins*

Some of the earliest fish on the planet had a bizarre appearance. Unfortunately, we cannot gain any insight into their coloration and patterning from fossils.

Skeletons from the past

Sharks, along with their close relatives such as rays and skates, are known as cartilaginous fish, because their skeleton is predominantly cartilage, coated with bone for extra support. By contrast, the skeleton of bony fish or teleosts, which form the class Osteichthyes, is made up entirely of bone. Fossil records date them as living approximately 400 million years ago. Since then, they have undergone remarkable diversification, and today there are more than 20,000 different species, making them the largest group of fish on the planet and the biggest class of vertebrates.

There are three subdivisions, of which the oldest are the actinopterygians. They are often called ray-finned fish, and are characterized by bony spines in the fins. Originally, these fins were largely immobile, but changes in the bone structure in later osteichthyans, such as *Perleidus* from the Triassic period (about 240 million years ago) ensured much greater mobility.

SCALES

The earliest fish had a protective shield on their heads and relatively large scales on their bodies, but as the actinopterygians developed, marked changes began to appear. The protective head armour gradually divided into smaller scales and those on the body became more flexible, assisting the fish's swimming ability. This evolutionary adaptation began with *Moythomasia*, which had interlacing scales (staggered, like the bricks in a brick wall) that gave it highly flexible yet rigid protection.

The emergence of modern fish

Unlike actinopterygians, the fins of sarcopterygian bony fish were equipped with muscles. This was a vital distinction, and a feature that can still be seen in lungfish, one of the few survivors of the group. Lungfish can breathe atmospheric air directly, rather than relying entirely on their gills. It is thought that amphibians probably evolved from sarcopterygians; the muscular fins provided the means for movement out of the water, and so began colonization of the land.

While only seven species of sarcopterygian or lobe-finned fish remain, there are more than 21,000 descendants of the actinopterygians. By the Eocene era, roughly 66 million years ago, teleosts were becoming established in fresh water, and some types are obvious ancestors to contemporary fish. *Hypsidoris*, for example, was very like the catfish of today, with trailing sensory barbels around its mouth and protective spines on each pectoral fin. Some teleosts were giants of 4m (13ft) or more, and their descendants still exist. They include the bony tongues, which have bony plates in their tongues that are used like teeth to hold food.

The arowana (Osteoglossum bicirrhosum) *is a living descendant of the giant teleost fish of the past. It is greatly prized in Asia as a symbol of wealth and longevity.*

Breathing and buoyancy

With their heavy body armour, the earliest fish were slow swimmers and lived close to the bottom of rivers or seas. As they evolved, however, they became more active, and so needed more oxygen – just as a human might gasp for breath after a sprint. Increased activity also made buoyancy control more important so that the fish could adjust their depth in the water.

Just as we depend on lungs to let us breathe in oxygen from air, most fish have gills to take in oxygen dissolved in water. In cartilaginous fish, the outside of the gills take the form of slits on either side behind the head, whereas in bony fish, they are covered by a flap called the operculum.

How the gills work

Fish take in water through the mouth. The water then passes over the gills where oxygen is absorbed into the bloodstream. At the same time, carbon dioxide from the body diffuses into the water. In cartilaginous fish, this deoxygenated water is then expelled from the body via the gill slits; in bony fish, the process is more complicated. While water is taken in through the mouth, the operculum and its membrane seal off the gills internally. As the water passes through the gill network, the operculum is raised to let the water out.

DIFFERENT BREATHING TECHNIQUES

The evolution of fish-breathing apparatus branched in diverse directions. Perhaps most remarkable are the lungfish (family Ceratodiformes), which have changed relatively little in the 400 million years since they first appeared. The African and South American species inhabit regions where stretches of water commonly dry out during seasonal droughts. When this happens, these fish survive by breathing atmospheric air directly, rather than relying on their gills. It is inhaled through a pair of nostrils located on either side of the mouth, then passes through the mouth into the lungs.

These extraordinary fish are also able to absorb oxygen through their skin, in a similar way to amphibians. Both African and South American lungfish will survive periods out of water, unlike their Australian relative, which has only one lung. As the water level falls, they burrow down into the mud. The African species actually secrete a cocoon of protective mucus around themselves.

When breeding, male lungfish develop filaments on their pectoral fins, which enable them to absorb oxygen from the water so that they can remain with the eggs, rather than having to breathe atmospheric air. Once the young lungfish

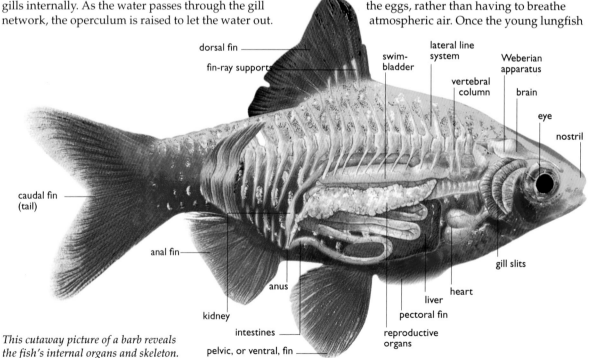

dorsal fin

fin-ray supports

swim-bladder

lateral line system

vertebral column

Weberian apparatus

brain

eye

nostril

caudal fin (tail)

anal fin

anus

kidney

intestines

pelvic, or ventral, fin

reproductive organs

pectoral fin

liver

heart

gill slits

This cutaway picture of a barb reveals the fish's internal organs and skeleton.

The labyrinth organ is an enlargement of the gill areas. It carries hundreds of blood vessels to absorb oxygen directly from atmospheric air.

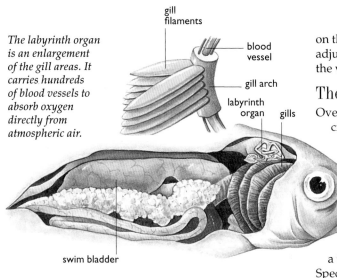

gill filaments

blood vessel

gill arch

labyrinth organ   gills

swim bladder

emerge from the eggs, they have external gills, rather like newt tadpoles, for up to six months after hatching.

Some fish have to obtain oxygen from stagnant water that is low in oxygen and so have evolved other means of respiration to compensate when their gills are unable to function effectively. Many catfish, such as the armoured catfish (*Hoplosternum* species), have accessory respiratory organs. The fish come to the surface and gulp down atmospheric air, from which oxygen is then extracted in the hind gut of the intestinal tract. Snakeheads (*Channa* species) have an air-sac bladder near the gills, which enables them to absorb atmospheric air.

The labyrinth organ

Some fish have a means of taking in additional oxygen via the labyrinth organ, a maze-like structure that is located just behind the gills. It is present in gouramis and most other anabantoid fish, which are commonly found in stretches of water that may have a low oxygen content. Oxygen from the air can be absorbed directly into the bloodstream from the labyrinth organ, and some members of this family, such as the spotted climbing perch (*Ctenopoma acutirostre*) even rely on this source of oxygen to keep them alive out of the water. These particular fish may sometimes be encountered moving across land, propelling themselves with their powerful pectoral fins.

CONTROLLING BUOYANCY

As fish started to move off the bottom and occupy other levels in the water, they began to evolve ways of altering their degree of buoyancy so they could control their depth. Early osteichthyans had a pair of air sacs

on the underside of the body which enabled them to adjust their level in the water by reducing or increasing the volume of air trapped here.

The swim-bladder

Over time, these air sacs fused in ray-finned fish, to create an organ known as a swim-bladder. In teleost fish, it is located in the upper body, connecting to the intestine. The importance of the swim-bladder becomes especially apparent when it stops functioning normally (see page 98), impeding the fish's swimming ability and making it hang at an abnormal angle in the water.

In some fish, the swim-bladder has become a totally separate organ, functioning independently. Special gas glands at the front of the swim-bladder enable carbon dioxide from the blood to enter it, increasing the gaseous pressure so the fish rises in the water. Conversely, the pressure may be reduced by gas being absorbed back into the blood towards the rear of the swim-bladder, like adding or releasing air from a hot air balloon to make it go up or down.

By helping to keep the fish afloat, the swim-bladder serves to reduce the fish's energy requirement. Cartilaginous fish such as sharks which lack a swim-bladder are forced to remain close to the bottom or must be powerful swimmers, in order to maintain their position in the water without sinking.

LUNGFISH

Modern lungfish live in freshwater but some types (*Propterus* species) can survive for periods entirely out of the water. Their retreat is prompted by a fall in water levels during times of drought, when they excavate a mud burrow in which to take refuge. This burrow provides a passage for fresh air to reach the fish, which remain buried until the rains return.

Fish senses

As with other creatures, fish have senses that have evolved in response to their environment. The constraints of life in the world of water mean that fish sensory organs have adapted in very particular ways. For example, water deadens sound waves, so fish rely less on their hearing than do land-bound vertebrates.

HEARING

Fish lack the sophisticated hearing apparatus of mammals, using their swim-bladder to pick up sounds. As a result, they can only hear frequencies in the general range of 100–1500 Hz, depending on species. Compare this with the human hearing range, which usually extends from 20–20,000 Hz.

In most cases, the swim-bladder lies alongside the fish's inner ear, transmitting the sound by direct contact. In the case of the Cypriniformes however, which include barbs, rasboras, and danios, the swim-bladder is joined directly to the inner ear by means of a series of bones known as the Weberian apparatus. This consists of up to four pairs of bones derived from the vertebral column, which act rather like those in our own ears, transmitting sound or pressure changes registering on the swim-bladder to the fish's inner ear. There is a similar system in catfish of the family Siluriformes.

Making sounds

Although fish have no larynx, some types can produce sounds that seem to be used for communication. Those with pharyngeal teeth may grate their teeth for this purpose. Some fish rub bony parts of their fins together, and the resulting sounds are in some cases amplified by the swim-bladder. Loaches forming the family Cobitidae can make a noise using air that they have swallowed to create flatulence!

SIGHT

The environment where fish are found in the wild has a significant impact on their eyesight. Species that typically inhabit clear stretches of water have good eyesight, enabling them to detect possible sources of food and signs of danger at an early stage.

Conversely, fish living in murky waters, such as many catfish, which are also nocturnal by nature, rely less heavily on their sense of sight, and their eyes are usually small. The blind cave fish (*Astyanax fasciatus mexicanus*), which occurs in a group of underground caves in Mexico, has lost its sight entirely. Despite this,

it suffers no obvious handicap, having evolved to live in its darkened, subterranean world. It represents an adapted, localized population of fish with normal eyes, which occur in nearby rivers. Blind cave fish fry hatch with functional eyes, but as these are not needed in the darkness of the caves, the eyes become covered by skin as they grow older.

In general, a fish's vision is adapted to seeing things close up rather than looking into the distance. The relative opacity of water, compared with that of air makes long distance vision difficult. To compensate, some fish rely on additional sensory organs, such as barbels (see right) or the lateral line (see box, below right), so that they are alert to other creatures and objects in the vicinity without having to come into direct contact with them.

The four-eyed fish

As you might expect, fish that live close to the water's surface have the most highly developed vision. They need to be alert to possible danger from above, as well as to food at or just above the water's surface. The eyes of the four-eyed fish (*Anableps anableps*) are divided into two halves, with the two parts of each eye functioning independently. These fish have flattened heads, so that they can see above the water with only their eyes protruding above the surface.

Although the eyes are divided, the lens in each eye is not. This enables these fish to detect danger out of the water while also as concentrating on their immediate surroundings under water.

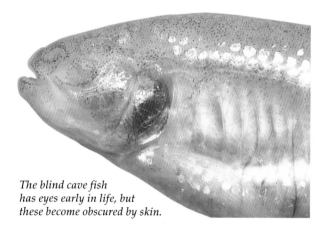

The blind cave fish has eyes early in life, but these become obscured by skin.

BARBELS

These auxiliary sensory organs are equivalent to fingers, enabling fish to probe for food in the substrate under conditions of poor visibility. They are most common in fish that live at this level, particularly in catfish, cyprinids, and loaches. Barbels may vary quite widely in shape, even between members of the same family. Predatory species of catfish, which may also occupy mid-water levels, tend to have longer barbels than more sedentary and herbivorous types. Some fish have straight barbels, while others may have a feathery, branched structure, notably the bristlenose catfish (*Ancistrus* species); here, the barbels are also a useful indicator of gender – branching occurs only on male fish.

The barbels of this Asiatic glass catfish (Kryptopterus bicirrhis) *are hypersensitive feelers, helping fish find food especially in murky water or relative darkness.*

TASTE

Fish respond to the four basic components of taste: salty, bitter, sweet, and sour. As well as having taste-buds inside the mouth, some fish are also able to taste with their barbels or even with their lips, which evidently helps them to determine if an item is edible before they eat it. Less obviously, there may also be taste-buds over the surface of their bodies. It is believed that these may have evolved to provide the fish with an indication of the degree of salinity in the water, for example, rather than as a means of distinguishing food items.

SHOCK TACTICS

While some fish produce electricity to stun prey and protect themselves from attack, elephant-nosed fish (*Gnathonemus petersi*) use electricity to light their way. They can generate a weak current to help them navigate in the dark and locate others of their kind which may be hidden from view in water with dense vegetation.

About 250 types of fish can generate electricity in this way from special muscle masses. Elephant-nosed fish increase their electrical impulses in response to a drop in water quality; as a result, some German water companies have used them to monitor samples.

THE LATERAL LINE

This highly sophisticated sense organ acts rather like radar, providing the fish with a constantly updated picture of its surroundings: waves of water bounce off objects in the vicinity, transmitting vibrations via the lateral line to the fish's nervous system and so to the brain. In some species, such as blind cave fish, it has become an effective substitute for eyesight, enabling them to swim without colliding with rocks or other underwater obstructions.

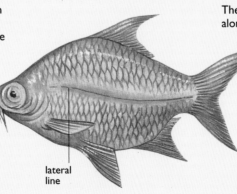

lateral line

The lateral line runs roughly midway along each side of the fish, and in some species it may be visible as a slightly paler area. It consists of a mucus-filled canal or tube, which is connected to sensory cells over the fish's body, extending around the eyes and mouth in some cases. These sensory cells are able to detect even tiny changes in pressure as vibrations, and then convey the information to the brain via the nerve network.

Osmosis

Think of what happens when you pour boiling water on a teabag – the water in the cup starts to become tea-coloured and the tea in the bag becomes saturated with water. This is an exaggerated picture to describe the basic principle of osmosis, the way in which differing concentrations of salts on either side of a porous membrane tend naturally to even out. Fish have adapted to help counteract this tendency, according to whether they inhabit salt or fresh water.

Marine fish

This natural process of osmosis would put fish that live in a salty water at risk of absorbing too much salt from the sea consequently losing fluid from their own bodies, leading to dehydration. Marine fish have therefore managed to minimize this potential water loss by producing very little urine. Although they drink large volumes of water, rather than absorbing the dissolved salt, they can pass it through the intestinal tract and out of the body. Although there is a tendency for the gills to absorb salt, the cells here actively excrete it.

The same risk may affect fish in brackish water – where sea and fresh water mix, such as in estuaries – but these fish can adjust over time (see box, below). Those from a stable marine environment, such as a coral reef, are unable to adapt to a change in water conditions, however. When buying fish, bear in mind that although certain groups, such as pufferfish, are found mostly in marine habitats, they do include some types, such as the green pufferfish (*Tetraodon fluviatilis*), that live in fresh water.

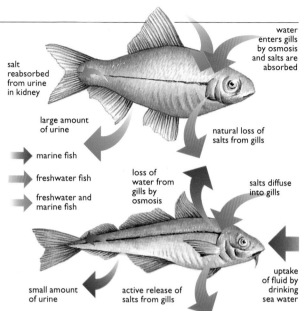

water enters gills by osmosis and salts are absorbed

salt reabsorbed from urine in kidney

large amount of urine

natural loss of salts from gills

marine fish

freshwater fish

freshwater and marine fish

loss of water from gills by osmosis

salts diffuse into gills

small amount of urine

active release of salts from gills

uptake of fluid by drinking sea water

In the case of freshwater species (top), water loss from the body due to the effect of osmosis may be problematic, and levels of vital body salts must be maintained. The situation is reversed in marine and brackish water species (bottom).

Freshwater fish

Freshwater fish face the opposite problem from marine species. The relatively high concentration of salts in their bodies, compared with the lower levels present in the water, means that their body salts would tend to be depleted by osmosis and fresh water would enter the

ADAPTING TO CHANGING CONDITIONS

Fish that live in river estuaries and other habitats where salinity may vary can adapt to differing conditions. When buying these fish, try to ascertain the water conditions in which they are being kept so that you can replicate these in your own aquarium. For example, some freshwater fish such as mollies (*Poecilia* species) are sometimes found in brackish water. In unsuitable water conditions, fish are more likely to succumb to opportunistic infections, such as fungus. Those moved from brackish into fresh water are particularly vulnerable, as their bodies have not been allowed to adapt gradually to the change in salinity. Unlike other members of the pufferfish family, green pufferfish (*Tetraodon fluviatilis* as shown) can be found in fresh water.

The basic circulation of a fish is like that of other vertebrates, with the heart acting as pump.

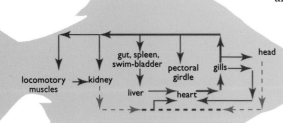

locomotory muscles → kidney

gut, spleen, swim-bladder

pectoral girdle

liver → heart

gills

head

Venous circulation (deoxygenated blood) is shown in blue, the arterial portion (oxygenated blood) in red.

body to dilute the higher level of salt. This exchange would ultimately have fatal consequences. To overcome the problem, freshwater fish produce large amounts of dilute urine, preventing the tendency for water to build up within their bodies. Although surrounded by fresh water, they do not increase their fluid load by drinking.

The urinary system

The basic structure of the fish's urinary system does not differ greatly from that of mammals. It includes the kidneys, which clean and filter the blood, and tubes called ureters which convey urine to the bladder for storage until it is excreted. Most bony fish have two types of kidney, known collectively as the opisthonephros, which are quite different in structure from those of mammals.

Freshwater fish need to retain salts in their body, so these chemicals are actively reabsorbed through the walls of the kidney tubules. Despite this, the fish's body still loses salts partly due to osmosis occurring in the gills. Not only is water taken up here, but salts diffuse out; in order to maintain the correct balance within the body, the fish has to have an active uptake of salt from the water.

The blood and heart

A fish's circulatory system includes the heart and blood vessels and operates in a similar way to that of mammals, although it is simpler in structure. As in

human blood, there are red and white blood cells, which function in a parallel way to our own. In fish, the red blood cells carry oxygen around the body and transport carbon dioxide back to the gills, while white blood cells help to protect against infections. The blood is pumped around the body by the heart, which is located in the lower half of the fish's body between the gills and the pectoral fin. A fish's heart is less powerful than that of the higher vertebrates, and has a relatively simple structure, being in the shape of an S-bend. Deoxygenated blood returns from the body via the veins and into the first chamber of the heart, called the atrium, before flowing into the muscular-walled ventricle. The contractions here force the deoxygenated blood back into the arterial system, via the gill arch arteries and so through the gills where the blood is reoxygenated to continue its passage around the body.

Heat regulation

Unlike humans, fish are cold-blooded, or poikilothermic, and so are unable to control their body temperature independently of their surroundings (see warning box, below). This is partly a reflection of their relatively sluggish circulatory system. Each type of fish has a preferred temperature range, although this may be surprisingly wide: for example, certain cichlids are found in lakes in the African Rift Valley where the water temperature may be as low as 5°C (40°F) for some parts of the year, and they survive without problems under these conditions.

Changes to the average figure may be necessary in some cases, to encourage spawning activity for example. In tropical areas such as the Amazon basin, the onset of the rainy period lowers the temperature of the river water and stimulates breeding behaviour.

WARNING

It is important that any changes to water temperature in an aquarium are carried out gradually, so that the fish can adjust to it. Tropical fish can adapt to a range of water temperatures, although typically their water should be kept within the range of 21–26°C (70–80°F). They can survive a degree of chilling outside their normal preferred range, but the resulting stress tends to make them more vulnerable to fungal infections.

Body shape and fins

One of the reasons fish are so absorbing to watch is because of the tremendous diversity in their shapes. Of course, though we are lucky enough to enjoy this, it is hardly for our benefit. Body shape influences how fish move and reveals much about their lifestyle. This is important when you are setting up an aquarium, because fish occupy different areas of water depending on type; this will affect your selection if you want to create a community aquarium with mixed species.

Near the surface

Some fish, such as hatchetfish forming the cyprinid family Gasteropelecidae, live just below the surface. They are characterized by their relatively straight backs and upturned mouths. Hatchetfish also have a very narrow body shape, which means they offer little water resistance, so do not have to battle against the current even if it is strong. A further adaptation to life in this area of water is the position of their pectoral fins, which are high, just below the eyes and away from the ventral edge of their bodies. These fins can even serve as wings, allowing them to glide up to 1.2m (4ft) above the water's surface if danger threatens them from below.

In the middle

The mid-water area is home to many shoaling fish, such as various tetras. These fish typically have a fairly symmetrical body and a powerful tail, making them first-rate swimmers. Although living in shoals provides some protection against predators, each individual depends on its ability to escape danger, and stragglers are likely to be easily caught.

A number of these fish, such as the spectacular cardinal tetra (*Cheirodon axelrodi*) are highly coloured, or have striking markings around their eyes, as in the glass tetra (*Moenkhausia oligolepis*). These patterns actually aid the fish's survival by breaking up its outline visually (sometimes known as disruptive patterning), so that it may be overlooked by a predator. Also, a predator drawn to the eye markings will be much more evident than one approaching from behind, giving the fish more opportunity to escape.

Not all fish occupy fast-flowing, open stretches of water. In reedy areas, a streamlined, torpedo-like shape would be a distinct disadvantage. In this kind of setting, the elongated, flattened shape of species such as angelfish (*Pterophyllum* species) is much more practical, enabling them to weave easily in and out of the reeds.

Studying a fish's body shape gives clues to its habits and behaviour. This hatchetfish has an upturned mouth and thin body, indicating that it lives and feeds near the surface.

The more streamlined shape of this tetra suggests that it is a shoaling fish, with a powerful swimming action. Such fish tend to inhabit the mid-water level, though they may feed elsewhere.

With a flat underside and a downturned mouth, Corydoras catfish are typical of fish that remain near the aquarium floor. They rely more on camouflage than speed to escape danger.

On the floor

Fish that live near the bottom often have a relatively broad and flattened body. They also tend to be sedentary by nature, rather than actively swimming like those that occupy the upper levels. Their preference for life on the floor is indicated by the position of the mouth, which may be virtually on the underside of the body, so they can feed on the substrate without difficulty.

Many types of catfish are bottom-dwellers, relying on camouflage to conceal their presence while they are resting. These fish often exhibit a variety of blotches and markings, providing disruptive patterning so that they are less easy for predators to spot. Some catfish have a very unusual appearance, such as the whiptail catfish (*Rineloricaria hasemani*), with its distinctive narrow body and whip-like filaments on the tail.

Loaches are another popular group of aquarium fish that frequent the lower reaches of the tank, even burrowing under the substrate in the case of the eel-like coolie loach (*Acanthophthalmus kuhli*). All species have a flattened underside, so they can swim close to the bottom and, like many catfish, they tend to be nocturnal.

FINS

Fish generally have seven fins: a single dorsal, caudal, and anal fin plus a pair each of pelvic and pectoral fins. Although most fish have this same basic arrangement, the size and shape of the fins vary significantly, reflected in the fish's swimming ability and characteristic style of movement. The main propulsive thrust is provided by the tail (caudal fin), its shape affecting the fish's speed in the water. Fish with cleft tail fins, such as the red-tailed black shark (*Labeo bicolor*), or with a lyre tail, where the cleft fin progressively narrows at the tips, are the most powerful swimmers.

Other typical tail shapes include the rounded form, such as in many cichlids, and the crescent outline. As the domestication of certain species such as guppies (*Poecilia reticulata*) has developed, so the natural shape of the fins has been altered significantly in some cases, becoming greatly enlarged due to selective breeding.

The function of fins

Fish use their fins rather like the flaps and rudders on an aeroplane, to manoeuvre and change their position. The fins themselves are composed of hard or soft rays, like flexible struts, webbed with tissue, which may be folded or extended with the aid of small muscles. The paired pectoral fins on the side of the

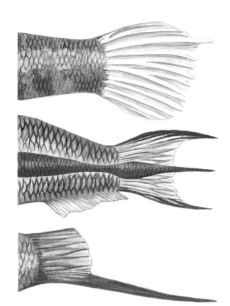

The shape of the tail varies widely and can be altered by selective breeding.

The tail may be an indicator of sex, as in this male emperor tetra with its extended rays.

The swordtail gets its name from the remarkable elongated tail of the male fish.

body help to maintain the fish's position in the water. Although these are often transparent and kept folded against the sides of the body which makes them hard to recognize, when extended out from the body, they also act as a brake.

The pair of small pelvic or ventral fins may also assist with braking. Their position on the underside of the body is more variable, sometimes in front of the pectorals, near the throat. Some fish have an additional fin on the back, between the dorsal and caudal fins. This small adipose fin is most commonly associated with members of the characin group (see pages 32–3), but may be present in other fish, such as the Corydoras catfish. It seems to have no real functional significance.

Courting and mating with fins

In addition to providing a means of locomotion, some types of fish use their fins for display and courtship. The raised, flowing dorsal fin and enlarged anal fin of the Siamese fighting fish (*Betta splendens*) makes an impressive sight. The male spreads his fins as an aggressive warning to potential rival males.

In some cases, the appearance of the fins varies noticeably between the sexes. For example, the male swordtail (*Xiphophorus helleri*) has a distinctive, sword-like extension on the lower edge of its tail. A further adaptation of male livebearers such as the swordtail has led to their anal fin being modified into a gonopodium, a tube-like structure used to convey semen into the female during mating.

Sociability and aggression

Fish, like people, do not always manage to live in harmony. In the restricted conditions of an aquarium, territorial and aggressive behaviour may be more pronounced; it is vital to do your homework before setting up your aquarium so that you choose fish that will live peaceably together.

THE COMMUNITY AQUARIUM

Thoughtful planning is vital to the successful establishment of a community aquarium. As well as working out how many fish the aquarium can safely accommodate, you must also consider which levels the fish will occupy, so as to avoid overcrowding. Check on their likely adult size, because they may grow considerably after purchase.

You can help to decrease levels of aggression among the aquarium occupants by making sure there is enough cover in the form of plants and rocks. This provides hiding places for young guppies, for example, out of sight of their rapacious elders who might otherwise eat them. Some fish use cover as a means of establishing territorial boundaries. In an open aquarium, with no vegetation, conflict is far more likely to arise, and although continual chasing may not directly harm weaker individuals, it does cause stress and so makes fish more vulnerable to fungus or other infections.

Predatory fish, such as piranhas (here, the red piranha, Serrasalmus nattereri), *can cause injuries with their sharp teeth, but remember it is not always easy to identify less obvious aggressors in a community aquarium.*

Small angelfish (*Pterophyllum* species) are often recommended for a community aquarium, but their trailing fins make them vulnerable to attacks by fin-nipping species such as zebra danios (*Brachydanio rerio*). Damaged fins may become infected, and the angelfish may die. If they survive and grow, however, then the tables are turned, and the larger angelfish may persecute their smaller tormentors.

The breeding period

Aggressive behaviour is often most apparent when the fish are in breeding condition, because they may turn more territorial at this time. An indication is the dominant male becoming more brightly coloured than his companions , and persistently swimming after weaker individuals and females. Their aggression is likely to focus on other members of the same species, but fish of a similar colour may also be harassed.

In these circumstances, you need to separate the fish, transferring the male and several females to breeding accommodation. Rather than setting up a separate aquarium, you may be able to use a tank divider for this purpose, keeping the male on his own if you do not want the fish to breed. Usually, you can remove the barrier after his level of aggression has declined; individual fish vary significantly in this respect, with some being much more troublesome than others.

With a few species, notably the Siamese fighting fish (*Betta splendens*), males must never be housed together. They are so aggressive that they will fight to the death, although they will live in harmony with other species.

The traffic light system

Before buying fish, always try to discover as much as possible about their sociability and behaviour. Some aquatic shops operate a guide known as the traffic light

---

WARNING

Although not all fish have sharp teeth, they can still inflict serious damage on each other in a determined attack with their strong jaws. The injuries may heal in time, but are likely to leave scarring. It may not always be possible to detect the aggressor in a mixed tank; for example, nocturnal catfish may not reveal their true nature if the aquarium lights are on, so take care to observe your fish at different times of day.

system. Fish marked with a green dot after their name are generally suitable for a community aquarium whereas those marked with orange may give rise to problems. Fish indicated by red dots are usually aggressive or have other particular requirements, such as preferring brackish water, which makes them unsuitable for the typical community aquarium.

Cautious introductions

Once established in an aquarium, fish establish their own territories and members of a group tend to resent new fish of the same species, even if they are compatible in other circumstances. The resulting harassment can lead to the rapid demise of the newcomers.

This problem may be especially apparent when you first set up your aquarium. Until the filter bed has matured and is fully functional (see page 52), it is best not to use the tank's maximum stocking density.

Rather than buying a few fish of each species and adding more later, it is often better to start with just one species and then add examples of another in due course. This is less likely to cause conflict, because members of each species can establish themselves as a separate group, without the newcomers having to settle into the existing hierarchy of their own species.

Above: The dazzling neon tetras (Paracheirodon innesi) *are small, sociable fish best kept in a group. They occupy the mid-water level and are peaceful fish for a community aquarium with soft, acid water.*

Below: To maintain harmony in a community aquarium, it is vital to select compatible species both in terms of temperament and space. Overcrowding tends to exacerbate territorial behaviour and aggression.

Reproductive behaviour

Tropical fish may be divided broadly into two categories based on how they reproduce. By far the largest group are the egg-laying species. The smaller group are the livebearers, which as the name suggests, produce live offspring. From the aquarist's viewpoint, it is usually easier to breed livebearers, because the critical stage of waiting for the eggs to hatch has been removed. It is no coincidence that livebearers such as guppies (*Poecilia reticulata*) and platies (*Xiphophorus maculatus*) have become so popular as aquarium fish; their offspring are larger than the fry of many egg-layers making them relatively easy to rear.

In the wild, very few eggs survive the critical period after laying until hatching, although this is only a few days at most. As a precaution, egg-laying fish usually produce many hundreds or even thousands of eggs at a single spawning. By contrast, livebearers give birth to only a relatively small brood, frequently comprising no more than 60–80 fry.

Mating and fertilization

The mating process is significantly different in these two groups of fish. With egg-layers, fertilization occurs externally: the male remains near to the female as part of the courtship procedure, then liberates his milt (sperm) over the eggs as they are laid. Not surprisingly, this rather haphazard method means that not all of them will be fertilized.

Livebearers have a more direct approach. The male's modified anal fin, known as the gonopodium, is used to channel the sperm from his body into the female's genital opening. The encounter is brief, but the effects are long-lasting, because a female livebearer can store the semen in her body. She will then be able to give birth to at least seven broods in succession, with the result that – in the wild – the females

probably only have to mate once to guarantee their fertility for life; in an aquarium, however, they will tend to mate repeatedly. This presents a problem for breeders who hope to pair up guppies, for example. Unless they are able to purchase young, immature stock, the females will almost certainly be fertile as a result of a previous mating, and so the parentage of the resulting young will be uncertain.

Early stages

Although the young fry develop inside the body of the female fish, there is no physical attachment like the umbilical cord and placenta found in mammals. The eggs themselves contain yolk which nourishes the embryos while they develop in the female, although in a few cases, such as the mosquito fish (*Heterandria formosa*) and related species, the fry receive nutrients directly from their mother, since their eggs contain only small quantities of yolk. Another unusual feature of this genus is that of superfoetation. This means that eggs develop at different stages within the female's reproductive tract. As a result, there may be an interval of several days between the birth of the fry.

Some fish, such as the discus shown here, exhibit pair-bonding behaviour. They are also devoted parents, cleaning the spawning site before the female lays her eggs, and then guarding it.

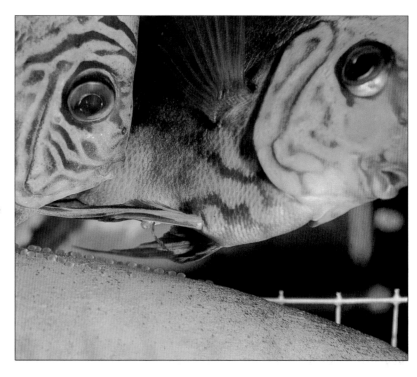

BUBBLE-NESTS

Many members of the anabantoid family, such as the male Siamese fighting fish (*Betta splendens*, shown here) construct a special receptacle for their eggs, in the form of a bubble-nest. Made by the male parent, these nests are formed from bubbles of mucus emitted by the fish. The bubbles congregate on the water's surface, where they often entwine around vegetation. The male then

induces the female to lay her eggs beneath this raft of bubbles. Once she has obliged, the male fertilizes the eggs straightaway, then collects them in his mouth before carefully transferring them to the nest. He makes a protective father, guarding the eggs for the few days until they hatch, then continuing to protect the newly emerged fry in their vulnerable earliest stage.

In guppies and other species where the egg sac remains intact until the end of the gestation period, the fry may be released into the water still partially wrapped in this casing. They soon manage to free themselves, however, and swim away on their own; their mother takes no further interest in them – other than as potential food!

In sharp contrast, certain egg-layers make remarkably dedicated parents, such as some of the cichlid species that occur in the Rift Valley lakes of Africa. The devotion of these mouth-brooders, such as the slender mbuna (*Pseudotropheus elongatus*), leads the female to collect her eggs after spawning. She keeps them in her mouth, without feeding at all herself, until they have hatched three weeks later. She then watches over her brood carefully and if danger threatens, she opens her mouth, enabling the fry to dart back in if danger threatens.

Pair-bonding

In many cases, male and female fish come together to mate and separate immediately afterwards, but some species may form a more lasting pair-bond. This is especially apparent with certain cichlids, such as angelfish (*Pterophyllum* species) and discus (*Symphysodon discus*).

Mouth-brooders keep their eggs safe in the female's mouth. Although it may look as if these fry are in danger of being eaten, they may be retreating into their mother's mouth for safety.

Signs of pairing are evident, especially if the fish are in a group. The two fish swim close together, with the male nudging gently at the side of the female. The pair then select a spawning site, usually a flat surface such as a piece of slate. They carefully clean the area, removing traces of algae and other debris, before the female lays her eggs and the male fertilizes them. The pair guard the site zealously, driving away other fish that may come too close and threaten their eggs. After hatching, the young fry continue to be watched over by their parents, who help them through the first critical days of life.

Development of the fry

In comparison with the relatively slow development of most mammals, fish have a much shorter lifecycle and so mature quickly. The incubation period varies for tropical fish eggs, but most hatch rapidly, because while still trapped in the confines of the egg, the young fish are too vulnerable to predators. Hatching generally takes place within 72 hours; if abnormally prolonged – because of low water temperature which slows the development of the fry – the eggs are more likely to be attacked by fungus. Under normal circumstances, unless the water is heavily contaminated, fungus is unlikely to be a significant problem, and only infertile eggs are likely to be affected.

The newly hatched fry

When the fry first emerge from their eggs, they still have the remains of the yolk sac on the underside of their bodies. This is a source of nourishment and is absorbed through the yolk duct which connects to the intestines. The young fish then remain mostly inert and hidden for several more days, until this built-in food reserve is used up. After this, they necessarily begin to swim freely and start seeking their own food.

At first, the fry feed on tiny organisms that are within easy reach in the water, gradually taking larger food

In the wild, the lifecycle of annual killifish (Aplocheilus species) is closely linked to natural seasonal changes. In effect, the entire adult population becomes extinct in an area, with only their eggs left behind to ensure the survival of the species.

PARENTAL CARE

In some cases, the adult fish remain on hand to watch over and even nourish their offspring at first, particularly if they have guarded the eggs. Breeding discus (*Symphysodon discus*) produce a special mucus secretion on the sides of their bodies, which the young fish can feed on as they start to become free-swimming. This helps to keep the family close together, enabling the adult fish to watch over their progeny for a further critical period of several days.

Certain *Mystus* species of catfish actually have a primitive nipple located on the underside of their body, from which their young suckle on a protein-rich secretion. Unfortunately, it is rarely possible to witness this behaviour because these particular catfish have proved to be difficult to breed in an aquarium.

items as they grow. Even in an aquarium where they are reared under identical conditions you will notice that some individuals grow at a faster rate than others. If this occurs, it is advisable to separate the larger fry, otherwise they may start to prey on their smaller companions.

Lifecycle and longevity

The lifespan of some fish may be a matter of just months, which obviously affects the speed of their development. In the case of 'annual' killifish, the fry must develop very rapidly. In the wild, these fish inhabit shallow pools that evaporate during the dry season under the hot sun, giving them only a brief period in which they can breed. If the opportunity is lost, the population will die out. These particular killifish, found in parts of Africa and South America, therefore mature within three months of hatching. They spawn as the water level falls, leaving their eggs encased in the mud at the bottom of the pool. The adult fish then die, but when the rains return, their eggs start to hatch, starting the cycle again.

Many cichlids are disruptive in an aquarium. Others excavate the substrate to create spawning pits where they lay their eggs, and corral the young fry to protect them from predators.

Problem parents

In some cases, particularly with pairs that are spawning for the first time, the parental instincts of the fish are thwarted. Once the eggs have been laid, all may appear to be proceeding quite normally at first, but suddenly, for no apparent reason, before they have even hatched the adult fish eats them. Immaturity or excessive disturbance appear to be common triggers for fish that normally have highly developed parental instincts to neglect or consume their eggs or fry.

When this occurs, it is obviously upsetting, but before long the pair should lay again and will often go on to reproduce successfully a second time. Do not worry if, as the time for hatching approaches, you notice the fish nibbling at the eggs. Under these circumstances, it is more likely that the adults are helping their offspring out of the egg casings, rather than trying to eat them. Some cichlids set up 'spawning pits' where the young fry can be guarded until they are able to fend for themselves. Although it is not possible for the adult fish to protect all their offspring, they can care for a significant number in this way.

Small fry have less likelihood of surviving because they are inevitably more vulnerable to predators. Some of the largest fry produced by aquarium fish are those of the four-eyed fish (*Anableps anableps*), which are at least 2.5cm (1in) long at birth. Not surprisingly, females of this species usually produce no more than four offspring at a time.

Mutations

It is quite common for some of the young fish to be markedly different in appearance from the adults, and they are often less brightly coloured. In a large group of fry, there may well be a few individuals that are clearly malformed. Not all mutations are necessarily bad, however; particularly in the case of prolific livebearers such as guppies, there may be a variety of natural mutations to basic characteristics such as coloration and fin shape in the newborn fry.

By separating out these individuals for selective breeding, it may be possible to develop new strains over a period of time. The breeding system used for this relies on Mendel's theory of genetic heredity. Each of the offspring will inherit one set of genes from each parent, so when one of the mutated individuals mates with a normal fish, the fry will carry the gene for the mutation, even though their appearance resembles the normal fish. At the next stage, if these individuals are paired together, a proportion of their offspring will bear the characteristics of the original mutant parent.

Careful breeding of this type has led to the wide array of colours now available, especially in the case of guppies and other species that reproduce very successfully. Unfortunately, problems may arise with selective breeding – for example, certain strains may die out due to infertility, possibly occurring as a result of pairing fish that are too closely related.

The guppies shown here, and other livebearing fish, produce live offspring rather than eggs. The relative ease with which they reproduce has helped breeders to establish a range of exciting colour and fin shape variants from natural mutations.

How the hobby developed

The ancient Egyptians were possibly the first to keep fish for purely decorative purposes, and over 1000 years ago the Chinese had begun to develop the idea of selective breeding in carp. Tropical fish-keeping, however, which depends on a heated tank, is a relatively new hobby. Until recently, the almost insuperable problem was obtaining the fish themselves as it was impossible to transport them without heat on long sea journeys. The second major obstacle was that without sophisticated electrical equipment such as reliable heaters and effective filtration systems it was difficult to maintain the water at the correct temperature and create a well-balanced environment.

Public aquaria started to appear in the 19th century. The first was established in 1853 at what is now known as London Zoo. In the early days, it was not uncommon to heat the water in an aquarium externally: the glass tank stood on slate, with a heater such as a bunsen burner beneath. It was only with the advent of widely available electricity, and the development of accurate heating apparatus for tanks, that tropical aquaria became a practical option. With these advances, tropical fish-keeping has grown enormously as a popular hobby during the 20th century.

COMMERCIAL FISH BREEDING

It was not long after the start of tropical fish-keeping on a wide scale that commercial breeding of fish began in earnest. This helped to guarantee regular supplies of fish, which, having been reared on farms, were likely to be healthier than their counterparts caught in the wild.

The first farm devoted to breeding tropical fish opened in Florida in 1926. Since then, the business has grown dramatically, with more than 200 such enterprises currently in existence, employing about 1000 people. The industry still remains centred in the area around Tampa, with similar businesses in the vicinity of Miami and Homestead.

Although fish-farming now represents a multi-million dollar industry in the state, it still remains at heart a family-oriented enterprise. In recent years, as aquarists become more experienced and ambitious, there has been an increasing demand for high-quality aquarium plants, which has seen this area of aquaculture develop alongside that of fish-farming.

Florida's favourable climate and connections with Central and South America – where many of the commercially bred fish exist in the wild – underpinned the growth of this business. At first, the trade in tropical fish was for the domestic market and fish were dispatched in special cans on the railroads to customers throughout North America.

During the 1940s, however, with the increasing number of private aeroplanes, Florida fish-farmers began to hire ex-combat pilots to transport fish by air, rather than by rail. Before long, air consignments were being dispatched regularly to Europe and other countries outside North America, which helped to trigger a massive growth in fish-keeping worldwide.

The sight of fish swimming serenely by seems to have an irresistible allure for people. Here, tourists stand transfixed by the constantly shifting scene at a public aquarium in Cape Town, South Africa.

The aquarium trade today

Commercial breeding of tropical fish has also become much more widespread, and US fish-farmers now have to compete with those from the Philippines, Hong Kong, and Singapore, where production costs are usually lower. This has resulted in increasing specialization, and Florida breeders now tend to develop and breed their own particular varieties such as gold dust mollies. Attractive mutations are carefully nurtured, because they could represent a fortune. Classes for such fish are staged at the annual Tropical Fish Farmers Association Show, which attracts buyers from all over the world each spring.

Florida fish-farmers have also focused on breeding the more difficult species in recent years. The techniques they employ are potentially highly valuable, because a single spawning may yield thousands of eggs and potential offspring. In some cases, breeders use artificial fertilization to guarantee the parentage of fish and ensure that a high percentage of the eggs produce fry.

The commercial farming of aquarium fish has now become a huge business, especially in Florida as well as in a number of other subtropical and tropical regions. The ponds shown here are being used for growing on fish prior to sale.

Management of the fish

The young fry are reared in indoor aquaria at first, before being transferred to outdoor ponds, where they can grow rapidly, feeding on the nutrient-rich algae and insect life. There are more than 20,000 of these giant rearing ponds in Florida alone, some of which are 47m (150ft) long and 16m (50ft) wide. Each may be home to up to 30,000 fish, which remain here until they are large enough to sell. This may take from two months up to a year, partly depending on the species concerned. The scale of this operation is huge, and the biggest fish-farm in Florida sells as many as 18 million fish a year.

Shipping

Once the fish are ready to be transported, they are netted and moved to temporary holding tanks, so their condition can be checked. They are finally transferred to heavy duty plastic bags, containing a relatively small volume of water, and oxygen is then pumped in, before the bags are sealed for the journey. These bags are packed in insulated boxes to maintain the correct temperature. The shippers pay particular attention to the ultimate destination of the fish, if necessary adding heat packs if they are being transported to a cooler regions, or ice packs if moving to a hotter climate.

In recent years, rising land prices have prompted some Florida fish-farmers to relocate closer to the Everglades, where they have unfortunately experienced serious problems with predators. Although the ponds are covered to exclude birds, raccoons have proved a severe menace, not only preying on the fish, but even gnawing through the water pipes. The introduced giant toad (*Bufo marinus*) has also created problems, exuding deadly poison from its skin into the water, with fatal consequences for the fish.

FISH FROM THE WILD

A small proportion of fish for sale in aquarium stores originates from the wild. Collection – and therefore availability – of such species is often seasonal, usually occurring in the dry season when the fish are easier to catch. In a number of areas, such as the Amazon basin, the sale of aquarium fish brings a valuable cash benefit to local communities, which would otherwise be forced to depend on a subsistence lifestyle.

Group profiles

Part of the irresistible appeal of fish-keeping is its tremendous scope. You can focus on a particular group, keep a mixed community aquarium of different yet compatible types, or even specialize in the various forms of a single species. Discovering more about the characteristics of the main groups will help you decide.

Factors to consider

The following section covers all the popular groups of tropical fish, outlining the pleasures and challenges of keeping each type. Before you decide which kinds of fish you want, you need to consider some key points. If planning a community aquarium, select fish that not only have similar environmental needs – water hardness, pH, and so on – but that are also compatible in terms of territory and temperament. In some cases, you can mix species from different families: for example, Corydoras catfish are suitable companions for tetras, which come from the same part of the world. Remember, native origins can be a useful indicator of which fish are likely to need similar water conditions.

Aggression and territorial matters

Some fish are predatory by nature, so obviously these must never be housed with smaller companions. Certain types are strongly territorial and will not live peaceably with others of their own kind in a small aquarium. If setting up a community tank, take care to select fish that will occupy different levels in the water. For example,

If you plan to house different species together, you must ensure they have similar requirements. Barbs, such as this cherry barb (Barbus titteya) shown below, need acidic water.

Cichlids from the Rift Valley, such as the auratus cichlid (Melanochromis auratus) below, require alkaline water conditions, making them unsuitable companions for barbs.

HOME FROM HOME

A vast range of aquatic plants is now available, so you should be able to create a truly themed aquarium, featuring plants that would be found in the fish's natural habitat. Remember to check the fish's diet; if you put herbivorous (vegetarian) species in a planted aquarium, you can't expect the plants to remain unscathed. Choosing tough plants should keep damage to a minimum, however. Some fish, notably the Rift Valley cichlids (see page 39) are usually kept in tanks with little or no vegetation, mimicking their natural surroundings.

hatchetfish live close to the surface, while other characins occupy the mid-level, and Corydoras catfish remain near the bottom. Structuring the population in this way helps to minimize friction between the fish.

Size

Before buying fish, always check on their likely adult size – some types can grow relatively large, and may then require separate and considerably more spacious accommodation than they had at the outset. It may not simply be a matter of obtaining a larger aquarium; you are likely to need a more powerful filtration system and heaterstat as well (see pages 52–5).

Breeding

As a result of widespread commercial breeding, some popular aquarium fish have gradually become more tolerant of a range of water conditions. This helps make them easier to maintain, and may also increase the chance of breeding them successfully in the home tank.

Reproductive behaviour varies, with a few species proving to be especially challenging in aquarium surroundings. The livebearers are the least demanding group in terms of breeding, a factor that has led to widespread interest in the development of different strains for shows and exhibitions.

The show and club scene

Keep an eye out in the specialist fish-keeping press for news of aquatic shows; these provide an excellent way of seeing new fish and meeting fellow enthusiasts to trade tips and advice, as well as giving you the opportunity to find out about up-to-date equipment.

There are also various national and international fish-keeping organizations devoted to specific groups of fish, such as cichlids. They produce regular bulletins, enabling members to keep in touch with the latest developments. Increasingly, the Internet is being used as an international forum for enthusiasts to contact each other and exchange information.

What's in a name?

Many people are daunted by the scientific names for fish (a system of classification known as taxonomy), but you may soon become fascinated once you understand them. The scientific name of any living creature tells you which species are related and yields other information, too. These names are also vital for international use, because they avoid problems with translation. Common names vary from country to country, and some species have more than one common name, which can be confusing.

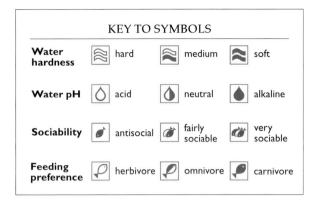

KEY TO SYMBOLS					
Water hardness	hard		medium		soft
Water pH	acid		neutral		alkaline
Sociability	antisocial		fairly sociable		very sociable
Feeding preference	herbivore		omnivore		carnivore

Like all life forms, fish are categorized into families, subdivided into a series of groups. For example, the cyprinids (family Cyprinidae) are split into a number of distinct genera, including *Barbus* (barbs), *Rasbora* (rasboras), and *Brachydanio* (danios). Each genus is further divided into species – approximately 1500 in total in the case of Cyprinidae. These separate species are different, but related – with some shared characteristics, such as barbels for example.

The scientific name comprises two or three parts: genus, species, plus, in some cases, subspecies. For example, the golden-striped rasbora is *Rasbora daniconius* (*daniconius* tells you which species of the genus *Rasbora* it is). This species includes two subspecies: *Rasbora daniconius daniconius* and *Rasbora daniconius labiosa* (the latter is slightly slimmer, with smaller fins); these features set it apart from the nominate subspecies, recognizable by the repeated species name. Names are sometimes abbreviated – *R. d. daniconius* or *R. d. labiosa*.

The golden-striped rasbora (Rasbora daniconius) *belongs to the genus* Rasbora, *part of the family Cyprinidae. The species includes two populations categorized as separate subspecies.*

Livebearers

The livebearers include some of the most popular tropical aquarium fish; this is partly because, as well as being highly attractive, they breed readily and are relatively easy to keep. This group includes fish as diverse as guppies, many with outsize, flamboyant tails, fiery-coloured platies, black and marbled mollies, and halfbeaks with their curious, jutting lower jaw.

GUPPIES

Named after the naturalist Robert J. L. Guppy, these were one of the first tropical fish to be kept in the early 1900s. Guppies (*Poecilia reticulata*) are now bred in a huge range of colour forms and patterns, and many have fancy fins or an especially enlarged tail.

For both the highly bred and the less showy wild forms, sexing is straightforward because females are distinctly larger and less colourful than males. It is often advisable to buy young fish, particularly if you want to breed your own stock, because adult females are likely to have mated (see page 20). If selecting adult fish, choose large females because they are likely to produce more fry.

SWORDTAIL

The swordtail (*Xiphophorus helleri*) derives its name from the male of the species; the lower part of his caudal fin (tail) is typically elongated, like a sword. The native form is green but this is considerably less striking than the various colour strains that have been developed through breeding, of which the best known and most common is the red variety. A curious fact about the swordtail is that females may sometimes switch sex and become male, particularly if old.

PLATIES

Another livebearer that has been developed in many different varieties is the platy (*Xiphophorus maculatus*). Like most other livebearers, platies are peaceful and easy to keep, and they are prolific breeders. These are relatively short, rotund fish and significantly smaller than the swordtail.

One of the most popular forms is the wagtail platy, with an orange body that contrasts strikingly with its black fins and mouth. Some hybrids have variations to the fins, most notably the hi-fin, which has a raised, enlarged dorsal fin. A slightly larger form of the platy occurs in Mexico. Sometimes called the variegated platy (*X. variatus*), this has a more elongated body shape and some forms are brightly coloured.

Some platies more closely resemble the wild species, having a dark, crescent-shaped marking at the base of the caudal fin – because of this, they are sometimes called moon fish. Sexing is easy: females have a fan-shaped anal fin, whereas that of the male looks tubular, and serves as the gonopodium for fertilization.

Less obviously striking than its highly bred relatives, even the wild guppy (Poecilia reticulata) *is an attractive specimen. It hails from South America and neighbouring Caribbean islands.*

Unlike the original, wild platy, many of today's domesticated strains are strongly coloured with red or orange, such as this coral sunset platy (Xiphophorus maculatus).

The velvety black molly (Poecilia sphenops) *contrasts well against the jewel-like colours of other tropical fish. The black form does not occur in the wild and is thought to be a hybrid.*

MOLLIES

As well as the well-known and popular black molly, other mollies have also become prominent in recent years. Many of the newer strains have enlarged dorsal fins. These are derived from sailfin mollies (*Poecilia latipinna*). In the wild, these fish are primarily silver, with bluish-green iridescence on their bodies. Various colour varieties are now firmly established, including the platinum which has no colour on its body, darkly marbled forms, and even the rather grotesque balloon molly, which has a distorted body with a high back and an outsize, balloon-shaped belly.

The correct water conditions are vital when keeping mollies, and it is advisable to add some aquarium salt to their water in the recommended amount. Mollies naturally inhabit brackish water, and they are more prone to fungus than other livebearers, especially if kept in pure fresh water. Check on their water conditions at the time of purchase, because they will be most vulnerable after a move to new surroundings. Black mollies in particular may also be susceptible to white spot (see page 104).

OTHER LIVEBEARERS

Although less commonly available, there are other livebearers which make fascinating additions to an aquarium. Halfbeaks (*Dermogenys pusillus*), which inhabit both brackish and freshwater areas, are most notable for their curious, elongated lower jaw.

They are sometimes called wrestling halfbeaks – owing to the males' habit of engaging in trials of strength, locking jaws with each other for up to half-an-hour. These jaws are quite easily damaged, so it is best to keep males apart, housing a single male with several females (easily recognized by their fan-shaped anal fin).

Gravid (pregnant) females must be left undisturbed; in favourable conditions, they may breed every four to eight weeks. Stick paper round the lower part of the aquarium, otherwise the young fish may try to swim through the glass at first, and damage their prominent jaw. You can also help to avoid this problem by using aquatic plants to demarcate the confines of the tank.

Among other livebearers that you may encounter is the mosquito fish (*Helerandria formosa*), which prefers relatively low water temperatures. The tiny males rank as one of the smallest fish in the world. Females have a relatively long birth period, producing their brood over the course of about two weeks.

An aquarium devoted to halfbeaks (Dermogenys pusillus) *can be relatively shallow, because these fish live close to the water surface where floating plants provide cover.*

Cyprinids

The family Cyprinidae includes many popular egg-laying aquarium fish, originating from Asia and Africa. They include the barbs, danios, and rasboras, many of which are suitable for community aquaria. Breeding these fish in such a set-up is rarely successful, however, because they tend to eat their eggs; it is advisable to use a separate breeding tank instead.

BARBS

These fish are generally very active and thrive in a small group, preferring an aquarium that is well stocked with plants. They live mainly in the mid-water and bottom levels of the tank. Many types have the characteristic whiskery barbels, the sensory organs that they use to help them find food at the bottom.

As well as the immensely popular rosy barb (*Barbus conchonius*), look out for the black ruby barb (*B. nigrofasciatus*), a slightly smaller species with smudgy black markings. When in spawning condition, you may notice that the red colour on the male's head assumes a more purple hue.

Tiger barbs (*B. tetrazona*) must be kept in well-oxygenated water, otherwise they congregate at the surface, and hang there vertically. Although sociable and not overtly aggressive, these barbs may prove problematic if housed with fish that have long, trailing fins such as Siamese fighting fish (*Betta splendens*), because they tend to nip the fins of their companions.

Some species of barb, such as the popular tiger barb (Barbus tetrazona), *are prominently banded, in this case with broad, black stripes crossing the body vertically.*

Another common barb with similar markings is the five-banded barb (*B. pentazona*), although in this case the bands are less contrasting. The males are typically more brightly coloured than the females, and the red markings on their fins are also more distinct.

Spawning in the aquarium is reasonably straightforward. Breeding has produced a domesticated form with elongated fins which is sometimes available, but there are relatively few variants of barbs compared with livebearers. Sexing may be easier when the fish are in breeding condition, as in the case of the rosy barb, which becomes much brighter at this stage.

DANIOS

Danios are relatively small, streamlined fish, with similar needs to those of barbs, although they tend to swim mostly in the upper water level, feeding at the surface. They are very sociable and should be kept in groups, especially when breeding. It is important to provide these fish with plenty of swimming space because they are naturally active.

Some forms are especially attractive, such as the popular zebra danio (*Brachydanio rerio*) with scintillating blue and metallic stripes along its body, and the well-named leopard danio (*B. frankei*), which is decorated with distinctive spots.

Sexing danios may be difficult, although males are usually more colourful. Zebra danios appear to develop strong pair-bonds, even in shoals, and are a good choice if you are inexperienced in trying to breed fish. With many danios, successful spawnings are relatively easy to accomplish, but you need to separate them from their eggs or they are likely to eat them.

Female zebra danios (Brachydanio rerio) *may lay up to 400 eggs. Hatching takes place about 48 hours later. It is best to use a shallow spawning tank, with a grid to protect the eggs.*

RASBORAS

In the wild, these fish are found in Southeast Asia, where there are approximately 30 species. Rasboras swim mostly in the middle and upper parts of the aquarium. They are best kept in a group; as well as showing them off to good effect, this also increases the likelihood of their forming natural pairs. This is important because it can be difficult to sex them, particularly outside the breeding season.

Many of these fish, such as the slender rasbora (*Rasbora daniconius*), are fairly subdued in colour, with a dark line running down either side of their otherwise silvery body. There are some striking exceptions,

however: keep an eye out for the red-striped or glowlight rasbora (*R. pauciperforata*) – its pale green upper parts offset the distinctive red line that extends from nose to tail on both sides of its body. Even more colourful is the clown rasbora (*R. kalachroma*) – it is pinkish-orange overlaid with a violet iridescence, and has dark blotches on its sides.

Another attractive species is the harlequin rasbora (*R. heteromorpha*); this pale silvery-gold fish has a dark, triangular patch on each side of its body, tapering towards the tail, and noticeably prominent eyes. This type of rasbora may be fairly difficult to breed, and you need to include suitable plants in the aquarium on which it can deposit its eggs. Gnat larvae can be a good conditioner for rasboras, although other live foods can also benefit the fish in this way.

OTHER CYPRINIDS

As well as the principal groups outlined here, several other cyprinids are also widely kept as aquarium fish. These include the red-tailed black shark (*Labeo bicolor*), which honours its more notorious but unrelated namesakes because of its streamlined shape and prominent, triangular dorsal fin. The striking red tail forms a vibrant contrast to its black body, making this lively fish an arresting spectacle. Unfortunately, these fish are aggressive towards others of their own kind, and breeding in an aquarium proves difficult. An easier choice is the related red-finned shark (*L. erythrurus*), which makes a rather more amenable tenant. It tends to be shy by nature, so make sure you provide it with adequate retreats such as rocks and suitable vegetation in the aquarium.

The harlequin rasbora (R. heteromorpha) *lays its eggs among cryptocornes and similar broad-leaved plants, so make sure these are included if you are setting up a spawning tank.*

The red-tailed black shark (Labeo bicolor) *is too challenging for most amateurs to breed in an aquarium because the fish are difficult to sex and tend to be aggressive towards each other.*

Characins

Many of these fish are brightly coloured or have a scintillating metallic sheen to their bodies, making them a delight to watch as they dart to and fro. As well as the highly sociable and popular tetras, this group includes the piranhas, made legendary by tales of their aggression and ability to strip prey to the bone in a matter of seconds. The characins include several families and number more than 1200 different species, mostly from South America, with some originating in Africa. One characteristic feature of characins is the presence of the small adipose fin on the back quite close to the tail.

TETRAS

When setting up an aquarium for tetras, you must ensure that you use soft, acidic water, which also encourages spawning. Many of these fish, especially the most dazzling species such as cardinal tetras, show to best effect when kept in shoals. They generally inhabit the mid-water level. Provide a well-planted tank with subdued lighting, to enhance their colour.

When buying neon tetras (*Paracheirodon innesi*), avoid choosing from tanks containing fish that appear dull and pale. Although bright lighting can make them seem poorly coloured, the pallid appearance may also indicate neon tetra disease (see page 105), a parasitic ailment for which there is no cure.

Far less colourful, but no less fascinating, is the X-ray fish (*Pristella maxillari*). This has an extraordinary,

The cardinal tetra (Paracheirodon axelrodi) *is an especially striking fish; it may be distinguished from the neon tetra by the red which extends the full length of its lower body.*

The marbled hatchetfish (Carnegiella strigata) *derives its name from the attractive markings over its body. It can leap out of the water, so keep the aquarium covered with a lid.*

transparent body, but may have black, yellow, and pale pink areas on the fins. The spinal column is clearly visible, while the internal organs are obscured in a silvery sac behind the gills. In spite of their apparently delicate appearance, these are not difficult fish to maintain in an aquarium. Other tetras also have semi-transparent bodies, although they tend to have some colour apparent. They include the black phantom tetra (*Megalamphodus megalopterus*), which has a distinct black blotch behind the gills on each side.

The bleeding heart tetra (*Hyphessobrycon erythrostigma*) is generally regarded as one of the more sensitive species. Initially, keep the water temperature in their quarters raised to around 28°C (82°F), then lower it gradually once they become established; this also helps make them more resistant to opportunistic fungal infections.

It is often wise to stock the aquarium with relatively hardy tetras, then add more delicate species once the water has matured and is more suitable to their needs. You can help them to settle in without problems by diluting some of this mature water with conditioned tap water (see pages 56–9) in the isolation tank, before transferring the fish to the established aquarium.

You may notice fin damage in certain tetras when you buy them, most often those with elaborate fins such as the emperor tetra (*Nematobrycon palmeri*), especially the males. Provided that the damage is not serious, however, then the fins should regenerate without problems, but watch closely for signs of fungus (see pages 102–3) during this stage.

This striped headstander (Anostomus anostomus) *owes its name to its unconventional head-down posture. This streamlined characin feeds by browsing on algae.*

Among the African tetras, the Congo tetra (*Micralestes interruptus*) is popular for its amazing iridescence. Be warned that poor water quality leads to a deterioration in the condition of its fins. Adding peat to their quarters helps to create favourable conditions, and spawning is quite feasible in aquarium surroundings.

HATCHETFISH

These strangely shaped characins live near the water surface – often looking as if they are suspended there – where they feed primarily on small insects. They may also jump out of the water to catch food, using their pectoral fins as wings, so keep the tank covered at all times. Include trailing plants in the aquarium because they like some degree of shade. Hatchetfish are especially partial to fruit flies, but will happily eat proprietary flake foods as well. When buying these fish, check for signs of white spot (see page 104), to which they are susceptible.

BLIND CAVE FISH

One of the most unusual of all the characins is the blind cave fish *(Astyanax fasciatus mexicanus)*, which has a highly developed sensory system (the lateral line, see page 13) to compensate for its lack of sight. If you want to create a striking exhibit, you could design a tank to mimic their native caves, using low lighting and slates firmly fixed in position.

PIRANHAS AND PACUS

Not all characins have an amenable nature – the group includes the notorious piranhas (*Serrasalmus* species). Although their aggressive nature has reached mythical proportions, piranhas should certainly not be housed with smaller companions, even of their own species, nor should you introduce another of their kind subsequently, because it is liable to be attacked. Aside from their feeding frenzies, these fish are otherwise surprisingly inactive and are generally quite easy to keep, although they are very unlikely to breed in an aquarium.

Like the piranha, the black-finned pacu (*Colossoma oculus*) grows quite large, so even a small group needs a spacious aquarium with a good filtration system. It closely resembles the piranha, but has distinctly different feeding habits – it is largely vegetarian.

In its native home of the Amazon, the black-finned pacu (Colossoma oculus) *feeds mainly on the fruits and seeds that fall from the rubber trees growing on the riverbanks.*

Anabantoids

Unlike other fish, which take in oxygen dissolved in the water via their gills, anabantoids have the extraordinary ability to breathe atmospheric air directly when necessary. They have adapted to survive in stretches of water that are often poorly oxygenated, with the aid of the labyrinth organ (see page 11); this has also given them their other name of labyrinth fish.

When breeding, most anabantoids build delicate bubble-nests: the male blows the eggs into a raft of bubbles of saliva he has formed at the water surface, and the nest itself is often anchored around floating vegetation. Pairs are often kept separately when breeding, because operating a powerful filtration system at this time would destroy the nest.

Some of these fish grow to a large size and are often caught for food in parts of their range, which extends through southern parts of Asia into Africa. When seeking aquarium stock, be warned that the common names may be confusing or misleading in some cases. For example, the gourami (*Osphronemus goramy*) may grow 60cm (24in) long, whereas the species often called the giant gourami (*Colisa fasciata*) is in fact unlikely to reach more than 10cm (4in) in length.

Wild Siamese fighting fish (Betta splendens) *are mainly brown, but domestic strains may be brilliant red, blue, or violet. The male, shown above, is typically much brighter than the female.*

The peaceful betta (*Betta imbellis*) has an attractive iridescence and is considerably less aggressive than its close relative, the Siamese fighting fish, but it is also less handsome, having fins that are much less elaborate. This fish likes a degree of cover and will thrive in a densely planted aquarium.

SIAMESE FIGHTING FISH

One of the most spectacular members of this group is the Siamese fighting fish (*Betta splendens*), which has been the subject of selective breeding in its native Thailand for centuries. This has led to the introduction of forms with elaborate fins, as well as those that are highly colourful.

As their name suggests, these fish are aggressive and males must be kept apart from each other, otherwise they are likely to fight to the death. They can be housed quite satisfactorily in a community aquarium, however, although for breeding purposes you will need a small separate tank for each pair.

Like other anabantoids, the female Siamese fighting fish does not lay the eggs herself in the nest. They have to be collected by the male after spawning. He then fertilizes them, puts them in a bubble-nest, and guards the site until after the fry have hatched. If you are rearing these fish, you should provide them with a suitable proprietary fry food or rotifers, because they have small mouths and may easily starve if supplied only with food items that are too large for them.

PARADISE FISH

These fish generally have vertical brown, metallic blue, and red bands across their bodies. Although they come from southern Asia, the paradise fish (*Macropodus opercularis*) is remarkably hardy, being unaffected by water temperatures as low as 10°C (50°F). Nevertheless, these fish are far more likely to breed in heated water, with the male constructing a typical bubble-nest. Make sure that the spawning tank is densely planted, to provide cover for the female, because otherwise the male may bully her in these surroundings. It may be worth adding some bogwood, which is often used as a point of attachment for the nest. The tank should also be covered, first to stop the fish leaping out, and subsequently to prevent chilling of the fry.

Spike-tailed paradise fish (*M. cupanus*) require similar care, but algae often features in their diet. These fish may vary in colour, with their body being mainly brown. The distinctive spike on the caudal fin may not be apparent in specimens that have been housed in poor water conditions, or in the company of fin-nipping species, but it should regenerate in due course.

GOURAMIS

Kissing gouramis *(Helostoma temmincki)* make a wonderful sight as they engage in the extended bouts of kissing from which they get their name. In fact, they are locking mouths in peaceful trials of strength. They use their prominent, thick lips to graze on algae, as well as for their more renowned pastime. The domesticated form is silvery-pink, while wild specimens have a greener hue. Take care to include plenty of vegetable matter in their diet, although even with this they may destroy aquarium plants.

The pearl gourami *(Trichogaster leeri)*, also known as the lace gourami for its characteristic patterning, is one of the most popular species. Like some of its relatives, it has long, thread-like pelvic fins, which are equipped with taste buds at their tips to assist it in finding food.

The behaviour of the kissing gourami (Helostoma temmincki) *never fails to fascinate, but their kisses are actually trials of strength rather than a sign of affection.*

Most fish do not utter audible sounds, but the croaking gourami *(Trichopsis vittatus)* is a notable exception. You are most likely to hear its distinctive calls during the spawning period, although these fish are not easy to breed successfully. As for related species, keep the water level low in the spawning tank, at about 10cm (4in), and increase the temperature to 30°C (86°F) in order to encourage egg-laying.

The moonlight gourami *(Trichogaster microlepsis)* is instantly recognizable by virtue of its tiny scales, which give it a striking silvery sheen. Include plant material, such as *Myriophyllum*, so they can incorporate it into their bubble-nests. Equally striking perhaps is the stunning golden form of the three-spot gourami *(T. trichopterus)*, one of various attractive colour forms.

Named for its distinctive white markings that resemble miniature pearls, the pearl gourami (Trichogaster leeri) *is one of the most colourful and widely kept of the gouramis.*

CARING FOR CHOCOLATE GOURAMIS

Unlike many of its relatives, the chocolate gourami *(Sphaerichthys osphromenoides)* is not a bubble-nest builder. The female is a mouth-brooder, like certain cichlids (see page 39), collecting the eggs in her mouth after they have been fertilized by the male. The young fry emerge from their mother's mouth when they hatch within about 19 days of spawning.

Chocolate gouramis have fairly specific requirements, especially in terms of water quality:
• Add a peat extract to the filter (see page 53).
• Make sure the water itself has a low mineral content, mimicking that of the gourami's natural habitat.
• Provide live food, which is especially important in the diet of these fish.

Killifish

Many killifish, which are also known as egg-laying tooth carps, have vivid colouring, some with eyecatching red, blue, or iridescent bluish-green markings. They have the advantage of being relatively small so may be kept in quite a small tank, and they will often spawn fairly readily. In general, killifish are not difficult to maintain, but they do have fairly specialized requirements, so are not usually suitable for inclusion in a typical community aquarium.

This group includes the remarkable annual killifish, so named because of their brief lifespan and unusual breeding cycle, geared to the seasonal changes in their natural habitat. These fish have adapted to ensure the survival of the species when the older generation are killed off all at once by drought, leaving behind their dormant eggs to hatch when the rains return.

ANNUAL KILLIFISH

These killifish inhabit shallow pools which dry up in the summer heat. As the water in their pools starts to evaporate, the adult fish are triggered to spawn before they inevitably die. Their eggs are buried, encased in mud at the bottom, and here they remain until the rains come, refilling the pools. At this stage, the fry emerge, developing rapidly because they must mature and breed before the water level falls again and they in turn die.

While these fish are at the mercy of their harsh environment in the wild, in an aquarium they may actually live for several years. Their eggs may also remain viable for several years, so unlike other fish, they can be purchased in the form of eggs, which are sold in peat and are easy to transport.

In an aquarium, you can encourage some killifish to breed as they would in the wild, but some types will happily lay their eggs among aquatic vegetation instead. One example of this is the gularis (*Aphyosemion gulare*), a killifish with a wide variety of appearance among individuals. Some captive strains now tend to be quite yellow, with purplish markings on their bodies, while others are partially blue, with red blotches. Gularis may be quite aggressive, so it is best to separate the males, housing one in the company of several females.

Walker's aphyosemion (*A. walkeri*), in contrast to gularis, is a dedicated substrate spawner. For these fish, you need to provide soft water conditions, mimicking those of the rainwater that fills their pools, while a layer of peat at least 2.5cm (1in) deep is recommended for the aquarium floor. To encourage spawning, the water level should be lowered; because of this, it is preferable to use an external heating pad placed under the aquarium, or at the back, rather than a tubular heater which could be exposed to the air as the water level falls.

Once the fish have spawned, they may be transferred to separate quarters, leaving the water in this aquarium to evaporate. Keep the surface just slightly damp – using water that you have first dechlorinated – with a plant mist-sprayer if necessary. After an interval of at least one month, you can flood the aquarium again,

The killifish called gularis (Aphyosemion gulare) *show wide variation in their colour forms, with males invariably being more brightly coloured than the females.*

Water temperature affects the colour of Walker's aphyosemions – they become paler as it rises. It also appears to shorten their lifespan, as it would in the wild.

Guenther's nothobranch (Nothobranchius guentheri) *are East African annual killifish with a fast breeding cycle; the young fish are mature after only three months.*

using soft, conditioned water. The killifish fry should then begin to hatch quite rapidly.

Among the other annual killifish that are often kept in aquaria are members of the genus *Nothobranchius*, such as Guenther's nothobranch (*N. guentheri*). They are frequently very colourful, especially in the case of males. As with other killifish, make sure that live food is a significant part of their diet. Including plenty of vegetation in their shallow aquarium should decrease the level of aggression among the male killifish. It is advisable to change their water regularly.

The eggs of these killifish often take longer to hatch than for *Aphyosemion* species: up to six months is not unusual. Allow four months before adding fresh water, and the fry should start emerging after about a month.

NEW WORLD KILLIFISH

Killifish are also found in the Americas. The male American flagfish (*Jordanella floridae*), which is found from Florida down to the Yucatan, has rows of red and blue-green spots, as colourful as the brightest of flags. They are more vegetarian in their feeding habits than other killifish, and they are also substrate spawners. Leave the male to guard the eggs, but separate the female, or she will eat them.

Pearlfish (*Cynolebias* species), which originate in South America, have a similar lifecycle to their African relatives. These are recognizable by their spotted appearance. Similar conditions as for African annual species are required, although the New World killifish will often tend to take longer to hatch.

It is worth drying out the substrate a second time once all the fry seem to have hatched, and then flooding the surface again, as more young killifish may well emerge. This delayed hatching of a proportion of the eggs is a natural feature, providing the species in a particular locality with a second chance of survival should there be inadequate rainfall at first, with the water evaporating before the fish can complete their lifecycle.

OTHER KILLIFISH

There are other killifish which inhabit permanent areas of water and breed in a more conventional way, rather than spawning in the substrate. These include other members of the genus *Aphyosemion*, such as the striped aphyosemion (*A. striatum*). This is one of the species that will benefit from the addition of some marine salt to the aquarium water, because this minimizes the risk of their succumbing to a fungal infection. Regular partial water changes are also helpful in this respect.

They typically lay their eggs on fine-leaved plants, doing this gradually over several weeks in the case of some species. The eggs should then be transferred to a separate tank for hatching, otherwise the young fry are at risk of being eaten by the adult fish.

Male dwarf Argentine pearlfish (Cynolebias nigripennis) *darken in colour at the onset of the spawning period. Female fish lack the spots and iridescence seen in the males.*

Cichlids

These fish have a wide distribution, with most hailing from Africa and the New World, and a few from Asia. Cichlids need varying water conditions, depending on type, so check carefully on this before buying. For example, cichlids from Lake Malawi, in the Rift Valley area of east Africa, require hard water; using coral gravel helps maintain the right water conditions, especially if you live in an area with soft tap water.

NEW WORLD CICHLIDS

Cichlids from Central and South America generally require soft water, in common with other fish from this region. Although small cichlids may appear quite docile, bear in mind that they usually grow fast, then tend to prey on smaller companions. Oscars (*Astronotus ocellatus*) are typical in this respect, although these fish are popular because they can readily be tamed.

Angelfish

With their elegant shape and beautiful markings, angelfish (*Pterophyllum* species) are much loved, but they are also not suitable for an average community aquarium. They grow rapidly, tending to outstrip their companions, and their trailing fins are often nibbled. Most popular are the angelfish itself (*P. scalare*) and the less common deep angelfish (*P. altum*), with its distinctive depression in front of the eyes. There are various colour forms, including an attractive yellow and silver variety.

Angelfish may be kept in shoals at first, but for breeding purposes, house pairs on their own. Increase the amount of live food in their diet to trigger breeding behaviour. They will sometimes breed in an aquarium, often using a piece of slate for spawning purposes. Like many cichlids, angelfish show a degree of parental care, guarding their eggs until the fry hatch.

Discus

The development of new colours has focused most strongly on the discus (*Symphysodon discus*); these have established a dedicated following, with rare colours in particular fetching large sums. This is partly because discus are sensitive fish, with highly specific needs in terms of conditions. They require soft, slightly alkaline, well-filtered water, but provided this need is met, they are not difficult fish to look after.

Breeding may be disappointing, particularly with young fish, which may well eat their eggs, but they should spawn again before long, usually with greater success. If buying young discus, remember that they may take up to nine months to attain their full coloration.

For angelfish, such as this deep type (Pterophyllum altum), *provide a deep aquarium, with plenty of upright vegetation so they can weave in and out of plants as they do in the wild.*

ASIAN CICHLID

The best known of the Asiatic cichlids for the aquarium is the orange chromide (*Etroplus maculatus*), which has a yellow-orange body with red dots and dark markings. Seclusion is important for this species to spawn successfully, and it is advisable to provide bogwood rather than rockwork for egg-laying sites. These fish often inhabit slightly brackish waters, so it is a good idea to add a little marine salt to the tank; this often serves to enhance their attractive coloration and reduce their susceptibility to fungal disease.

CENTRAL AMERICAN CICHLIDS

Many of these cichlids should be kept on their own, because the males often become large and aggressive. As they come into spawning condition, males may persecute females ferociously, so it may be necessary to separate them for a period to prevent injury. Larger cichlids, such as the firemouth (*C. meeki*) and the pugnacious Jack Dempsey (*C. octofasciatum*) – justly named after the famous boxer – are also prone to uprooting plants and even biting at the heaterstat; use an external type of heater for these fish as they mature.

One reason these fish cause such an upheaval is their habit of creating spawning pits in the substrate. The eggs are laid on rockwork and, after hatching, the fry are shepherded into these pits, where they are guarded by the adults during the critical early days of life.

AFRICAN CICHLIDS

Few fish are more devoted parents than the mouth-brooding cichlids from the Rift Valley lakes in Africa, such as the zebra Malawi cichlid (*Pseudotropheus zebra*). After spawning, the female collects the eggs in her mouth and keeps them there for roughly three weeks, without feeding herself, until the young hatch. They will remain close to her, darting back into her mouth if danger threatens, for a further week or so.

Many of the Rift Valley cichlids vary widely in appearance, which makes pairing difficult at times. For example, most zebra Malawi cichlids are light blue with

Like other Central American cichlids, the firemouth cichlid (Cichlasoma meeki) *can be aggressive, especially the males.*

Today's domesticated strains of discus (Symphysodon discus) *are far brighter in colour than their wild relatives, ranging from stunning blues to a recent bright tangerine-orange form.*

dark stripes, but there is also an orange form with black blotches; most of the latter type are apparently female.

Sexing is relatively important with these cichlids, because males are naturally territorial, and so several females are best accommodated with a single male. Some are monogamous, however, such as the stunning lemon cichlid (*Lamprotogus leleupi*) from Lake Tanganyika. Keep pairs apart from others of their own kind, as they will prove to be aggressive.

Cichlids such as the Malawi golden cichlid (Melanochromis auratus) *may vary considerably in their depth of colour.*

Catfish

They may lack the bright colours of many tropical fish, but their unusual shapes, varied patterning, and intriguing behaviour have made catfish one of the most popular groups of tropical aquarium fish worldwide. Widely distributed around the world, these fish may be found in a wide range of habitats; some inhabit fast-flowing rivers and others live in stagnant ponds. More than 2000 different species are already known and new ones are still being discovered. Many types can breathe atmospheric air, and you may notice them darting to the surface before they return to their preferred territory near the aquarium floor. There is a see-through type known as the glass catfish and even an upside-down catfish which makes a curious sight as it swims along, alert to possible predators above the water.

The most distinctive feature of catfish are their sensory barbels near the mouth – these resemble cats' whiskers, which is how these fish earned their common name. The barbels vary in size, and may be branched or feathery in appearance, depending on the species. Catfish use their barbels to assist them in locating food in murky water or after dark, which is when these fish are usually most active.

Catfish may prove rather shy, especially at first, but smaller species are an attractive addition to any community tank, while some bigger specimens make a spectacular display in a suitably spacious aquarium. A few species, such as the striking red-tailed catfish (*Phractocephalus hemiliopterus*) from South America, are predatory by nature so are not a good choice for a typical community aquarium. This particular species may grow to over 90cm (3ft) in length, so its size alone makes it unsuitable for the average tank.

Feeding

The feeding behaviour of these fish is interesting to witness. Most catfish have a reputation as scavengers, a characteristic that has endeared them to aquarists because they will sometimes eat the food leftovers of other tank occupants. They do certainly forage for food in the aquarium substrate, but it is important to feed them properly if they are to thrive.

By contrast with the foragers, certain types known as suckermouth catfish have powerful, rasping mouth parts which enable them to browse on algae that grows on rocks. They are also able to use their sucker mouths to anchor themselves in fast-flowing water.

CORYDORAS CATFISH

The best-known catfish for home aquaria are members of the *Corydoras* genus. These are small catfish, rarely growing beyond 10cm (4in) in length, and the pygmy catfish (*Corydoras pygmaeus*) certainly justifies its title, measuring barely 2.5cm (1in) even when adult.

These fish need a sense of security, so set up retreats and crevices using rockwork in the aquarium. Provide water that is neutral or slightly alkaline. Temperature is less significant but should be within the range of 19–26°C (66–79°F). Proprietary foods suit these catfish well, but they will also eat leftovers from other members of a community tank. All corydoras may prove quite disruptive in a planted aquarium because they tend to burrow into the sandy floor covering. Set the aquarium plants in pots to prevent them from being uprooted.

Females are generally recognizable by their larger size and paler colour. The bronze corydoras (*C. aeneus*) is one of the easiest species to breed in a home aquarium. Ideally, the tank should have a sandy bottom, and you can stimulate spawning by raising the daytime temperature of the water and then allowing it to drop slightly lower than usual during the night.

Females lay their eggs over plants in small batches of a dozen or so at a time. During the course of several hours, they may lay a total of about 200 eggs. After this, you should move the adult fish to separate quarters,

Among the most popular catfish is the bronze corydoras (Corydoras aeneus), which has a brown body colour with a metallic bronze-green sheen. Originating from the northern part of South America, it is now bred all over the world.

before they can eat the spawn. Hatching takes place about five days later, and the newly hatched fry should be reared on special fry foods at first.

The most free-breeding member of the group is probably the peppered corydoras (*C. paleatus*), so named because of its brown body markings. It was first bred in Europe in 1878, long before many such tropical species could even be successfully kept alive. Selective breeding has now produced various strains of this fish, even some that are pure white.

UNUSUAL CATFISH

One of the strangest of all catfish originates from southeast Asia. The glass catfish (*Kryptopterus bicirrhis*) has long, slender barbels, indicating its active nature. Its body is transparent, revealing its skeleton, but it also has an iridescent quality. These catfish tend to inhabit the mid-water levels and thrive when kept as a small group. In contrast to many other catfish, they are very lively, with their tails almost perpetually sweeping to and fro. A similar glass catfish (*Eutropiellus debauwi*) also occurs in Africa, although its body is decorated by black stripes running along its length.

Other African catfish that are often available for the aquarium include the *Synodontis* species, such as the upside-down catfish (*S. contractus*). Its markings appear to be the wrong way up but serve as effective camouflage. These fish spend much of their time swimming on their backs, grazing on algae on the underside of leaves of aquatic plants, although they also feed on the floor of the aquarium. Take care when

Many catfish live near the substrate and some rely on a degree of camouflage to avoid detection, such as the twig catfish (Farlowella gracilis) *from South America. Its brown body is so thin that it is also sometimes known as the needle catfish.*

SUCKERMOUTH CATFISH

Suckermouth catfish (*Hypostomus punctatus*) have a distinctive sucking mouth. They are fascinating to watch, and you may often see their strange mouths flattened against the aquarium wall as they try to feed.
• They feed on algae, so are helpful in keeping down algae levels in a tank, but you must provide enough vegetable matter or they will eat the aquarium plants.
• Include bogwood in their tank that they can rasp or use as a point of anchorage, attaching themselves with their sucker-like mouths.

catching or transferring these fish because, like other catfish, they have spiny fins, which may become entangled and damaged in a catching net. It may be better to catch the fish by directing them carefully into a bag in the aquarium. Upside-down catfish are good occupants for a community aquarium, but it is unknown for them to breed in such a setting. Some other *Synodotis* species are less suitable, however, proving too large for the average aquarium because they reach nearly 60cm (2ft) in length.

Miscellaneous groups

In addition to the principal groups of tropical freshwater fish, there are many other interesting and unusual fish that you may come across. These include the beautiful, such as the butterfly fish with its expansive fins; the reclusive, in the form of shy loaches; even the impostors, like the leaf fish, which mimics the form of a leaf. Perhaps most peculiar of all are the elephant-nosed fish (*Gnathonemus* species), which have an elongated lower jaw like a miniature elephant's trunk.

Elephant-nosed fish use their trunk-like appendage to forage for worms and similar creatures in the substrate. In an aquarium, a sandy rather than gravel base is therefore preferable, enabling them to root more easily. The aquarium should also be densely planted, and the lighting subdued. These fish have poor sight and are more active after dark, a fact reflected by their output of electrical impulses, which help them to navigate without colliding with obstructions.

BUTTERFLY FISH

Not to be confused with the well-known marine species, butterflyfish, the butterfly fish (*Pantodon bucholzi*) is unrelated and looks very different. It has a slender body, but its pectoral fins are greatly enlarged, resembling the wings of a butterfly. These graceful fish live close to the surface and may even use these fins as if they were really wings to help them glide for short distances out of the water. It is therefore particularly important to keep their aquarium covered at all times.

With its flowing, wing-like fins and decorative markings, the butterfly fish (Pantodon bucholzi) *is a beautiful sight.*

The extraordinary elephant-nosed fish (Gnathonemus petersi) *lives mainly near the bottom, where it searches for food with its sensitive, protruding lower jaw.*

In an aquarium for these fish, include floating plants to provide retreats for them at the surface. Butterfly fish will instinctively lurk here and ambush any insects that pass within reach, in or out of the water. They also prey on small fish, so should not be kept with livebearers.

Butterfly fish may spawn successfully in aquarium surroundings, provided that they are well fed with suitable live foods. Their eggs are unusual in that they float, making them easy to collect. Transfer them to a nursery tank, where the fry will hatch within about two days. Take care if you have a power filter in the aquarium, however, because some eggs may be sucked into the unit. If you want to breed these fish regularly, an alternative method of filtration is preferable.

Vibrantly striped, eel-like coolie loaches (Acanthophthalmus kuhli) *often lurk in vegetation or under rocks.*

Clown loaches (Botia macrantha) – *also called tiger loaches because of their colour and stripes – may vary in intensity of colour, depending on their region of origin rather than diet.*

LOACHES

The members of this group are nocturnal and generally shy. In the wild, they usually live on the bed of a river or stream, and in a tank, often stay near the bottom or lurk in vegetation. Dimming the aquarium light may encourage them to emerge from their hiding-places. Coolie loaches (*Acanthophthalmus kuhli*) in particular often prove rather elusive. Like true eels, they seek out refuges, sometimes disappearing from view for long periods. If you have an undergravel filter, make sure it is properly fitted in the base of the tank, otherwise these loaches will tend to retreat beneath it.

Another loach you may come across is the striking clown loach (*Botia macrantha*). Bear in mind that, although specimens on sale may be small, unlike other aquarium-kept loaches, the clown loach can grow quite large so will ultimately require a suitably spacious tank.

Confusingly, the zebra loach (*B. striata*) is sometimes also displayed as the clown loach, but in fact its alternating light and dark bands are much narrower. It is important to distinguish between these two species because the adults are very different in size and so have different needs in terms of space. In other ways, their basic requirements are similar, although regular water changes are particularly important with the zebra loach; it naturally inhabits fast-flowing waters, where there is no build-up of pollutants such as nitrates, so they are unaccustomed to dealing with them in their environment.

Take care when handling any loaches because these fish all have a small spike under each eye, which can get caught in the net when the loach is captured. If this does happen, disentangle it very gently so you do not injure the fish.

LEAF FISH

Some predatory species are not active hunters. Instead, they wait for their prey to come to them, relying on camouflage to disguise their presence. A typical example is the South American leaf fish (*Monocirrhus polyacanthus*), which may rest with its head pointing downwards, to enhance the impression that it is inert. This unusual fish even has a slender growth on its chin that looks like a leaf stem. With its large mouth, it sucks in any unwary invertebrates or small fish that venture too close.

These fish are not always easy to establish in a tank; try to ensure that they are feeding properly before buying, or they may succumb to fungus, especially if their new water conditions are not ideal. When netting them, avoid damaging the spines on the dorsal fins.

Once settled, leaf fish may breed successfully. The eggs are guarded by the male until the fry hatch; transfer them at this stage or they may be eaten by their parents. As they grow, separate them into groups of similar-sized individuals to prevent cannibalism.

The coloration of leaf fish (Monocirrhus polyacanthus) *varies to suit their background, altering from shades of yellow to dark brown, so that they do not alert unsuspecting prey.*

Preparing an aquarium

An attractive, well-planned aquarium can be a striking focal point in any room. Whether you want to keep just a few large fish or a traditional community aquarium, preparing the right environment has never been easier to achieve, thanks to modern technology – plus careful planning and plenty of patience.

Choosing an aquarium

Establishing an aquarium involves creating your own miniature ecosystem; it is worth taking the trouble to get the individual elements right so that they work together to form a well-balanced, harmonious whole. Although you need the aquarium fully set up, and the water conditions correct, before you obtain any fish, you should also have some idea of which fish you want before you buy the tank and equipment. If you decide to keep large species, it is wise to buy a sufficiently spacious tank at the outset. This saves money in the long term, pre-empting the need to replace the tank and equipment as the fish grow, and avoids transferring the fish unnecessarily and subjecting them to stress. Another advantage of having a large tank is that it makes it easier to maintain stable water chemistry.

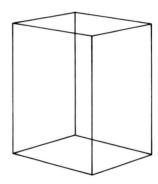

When choosing a tank, remember that a narrow, deep type typically accommodates fewer fish than a shallower one with a larger surface area. If using a tank with a low surface to volume ratio, it is especially worth including an air pump to ensure that the fish have enough oxygen.

Stocking density

As a rough guide, you can calculate how many fish a tank will accommodate from its surface area. To work this out, simply multiply the width by the length of the tank. For example, taking a typical aquarium with 30 x 90cm (12 x 36in) dimensions, this provides a surface area of 2700sq cm (432sq in). When calculating how many fish your tank will support, allow approximately 1cm of fish (length excluding tail) per 30sq cm of water surface area (or 1in per 12sq in). Our example aquarium would therefore accommodate fish with a maximum combined length of 90cm (36in).

It is usually the surface area that is used as a guide, because this is where oxygen enters the water and carbon dioxide diffuses out, so is vital for the fish. The water volume is also sometimes used for stocking density, and this is worth knowing in any event, in case you want to use a water conditioner or need to add medication for the fish at any point (see box, right).

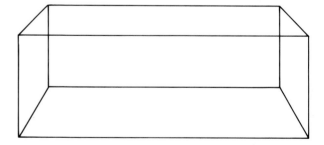

CALCULATING TANK VOLUME

Multiply the tank's length x width x depth (in mm), then divide by 1000 for the total volume in litres. Deduct 10% from this figure to take account of rockwork and other items in the tank. Allow 2 litres of water per cm of fish (roughly equivalent to 1 gallon per inch).
NB Imperial measurements tend to become complex in these calculations, so try using metric equivalents.

Territory and growth

Some people stock an aquarium gradually over several months, starting with only a very few fish. The downside of this is that there may be more problems with territorial disputes or disease introduced by new fish (see pages 76–7). Although fish in an aquarium may not grow as large as those in wild, you must allow for their growth, or they will soon be overcrowded. The stocking density figure should be regarded as a maximum; with aggressive, highly territorial fish, it makes sense to use a lower rate, to minimize potential conflict.

Starter kits

Go to a specialist aquatic store for a good selection of tanks. You may opt for a starter kit – an acrylic tank with built-in components including heater-stat and filter. Simply add gravel, plants, fill with water, add a water conditioner, and plug in. The system is then operational. These are obviously very convenient, and are usually quite stylish, so may be ideal as an initial set-up. One drawback is that they are often relatively small, so will only accommodate a few small fish, but they should be suitable if you want to keep guppies, or even a small shoal of tetras. You may prefer to buy the components separately, since this gives you more flexibility and probably a larger tank for your money.

Glass or acrylic?

• **Glass** Most ordinary aquaria today are made of glass rather than acrylic. Glass is far less vulnerable to scratches and retains its clarity, but it is not without its drawbacks. The most significant of these is its weight. A large aquarium is both heavy and cumbersome. It will also be especially difficult to handle if wet, because the glass may become slippery; always hold this kind of tank from beneath to reduce the risk of dropping it.
• **Acrylic** The main problem is that the surface can be easily scratched, which will obviously detract from the overall appearance of the aquarium. Over time, it may also become slightly discoloured, although modern tanks are much improved in this respect.

Silicone sealant

The advent of silicone rubber aquarium sealant has revolutionized tank design. There are now aquaria in a wide range of shapes and sizes and triangular units that fit into the corner of a room are especially popular. With some more expensive tanks, the bare glass edges are covered with a plastic surround. This protects you from the cut edge and may make handling easier and safer.

The silicone sealant binds the glass panels together, but does not actually set hard. It remains flexible yet strong, easily containing the force of the water in the aquarium.

Sealant checkpoints

• The sealant's effectiveness depends on its even application around the joints, so check that there is adequate coverage here, although problems are rare.
• If you need to repair a leaking tank, be sure to obtain a sealant specifically designed for aquarium use; similar products produced for other purposes may well contain chemicals that could be toxic to the fish.
• Check for algae, which may colonize the sealant and be hard to remove. If using a scraper to clean it off, take care not to strip off the sealant by accident.
• If adding any kind of chemical treatment to the tank, especially dyes, remember they could cause permanent discolouration of the sealant, so check in advance.

Modern perspectives

Built-in aquaria are becoming increasingly popular. This is partly due to the growing interest in large fish, which require not only a spacious tank but also a bulky filter system under or behind the tank. A large aquarium can be spectacular in the right setting, as a room divider, for example, but they are usually very costly to set up. Special toughened glass is needed for the tank itself, and you may need to make structural alterations in order to provide it with sturdy support, so seek specialist advice.

A less welcome trend has been aquaria made as actual items of furniture such as coffee tables and lamps. These may be awkwardly shaped for the fish, with vibrations and sudden changes in lighting levels likely to cause them stress. Cleaning and maintenance also tend to be problematic. A purpose-designed tank is better – as well as the conventional shape, there are now triangular and hexagonal ones available, too.

The aquarium substrate

The floor of the aquarium is usually covered by a loose medium such as fine gravel, known as the substrate. As well as looking decorative, this has some practical benefits: it provides a bed for biological filtration, an anchorage for aquatic plants, and – for some fish species – a place to forage for food or to make spawning pits. The choice of substrate medium depends partly on the type of fish you intend to keep and may affect water conditions. For example, while ordinary aquarium gravel is inert and does not affect water chemistry, coral gravel causes a rise in water hardness and pH – due to the limestone dissolving in the water. Some freshwater fish, notably Rift Valley cichlids, need these water conditions and so will benefit, whereas for other fish it would be harmful.

TYPES OF GRAVEL

If you use a very pale gravel, bear in mind that it will deaden the natural colour of the fish, making them look paler than normal. Coral sand is usually only recommended for marine aquaria, because its very fine particles may cause gill irritation in some freshwater fish. Coarser limestone gravel is safe in this respect, and may be mixed with ordinary gravel if desired, to reduce any glare on the fish. For fish that require soft water conditions, granite gravel is recommended; this should not contain any calciferous (lime-based) particles which would dissolve and make the water harder.

In some instances, a dark or undyed black gravel is a good choice, such as in an aquarium housing fish that normally live in subdued lighting conditions, but be wary of dyed gravels (see box, far right).

Size and quantity

You may come across gravel that has not been graded by sieving and so contains both large and small particles. Standard aquarium gravel is much more even in size, with a particle size of about 3mm ($1/8$ in), making it more suitable for a filter bed above an undergravel filter.

To calculate the amount of gravel required, allow roughly 1kg per 4.5 litres (2lb per gallon), based on the

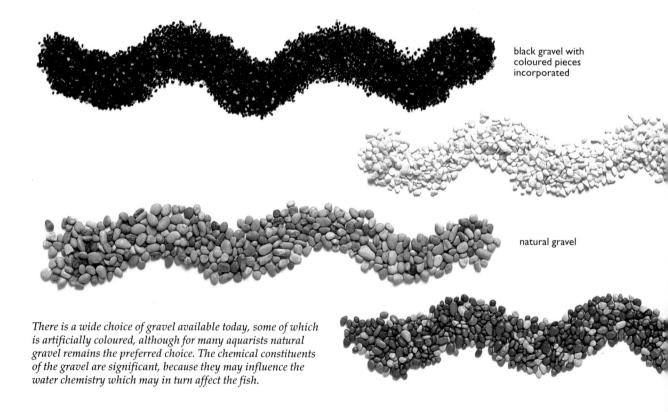

black gravel with coloured pieces incorporated

natural gravel

There is a wide choice of gravel available today, some of which is artificially coloured, although for many aquarists natural gravel remains the preferred choice. The chemical constituents of the gravel are significant, because they may influence the water chemistry which may in turn affect the fish.

tank's total volume. You will need a layer of gravel approximately 3in (7.5cm) deep above an undergravel filter, to ensure that it functions correctly, although this may be less with a different filtration method.

Preparing the gravel

Although ready-bagged gravel is often sold as pre-washed, it is still advisable to clean it again under a running tap. Without this precaution, very fine particles, mud, and other debris may form an unpleasant scum on the surface once you fill the new tank. There is also a risk that harmful microbes could be introduced in dirty gravel, so play safe by using a special, safe aquarium disinfectant initially.

First tip the gravel into a clean bucket, then make up the appropriate strength of disinfectant solution according to the instructions. Stir the gravel around in the disinfectant, then leave it to stand in the bucket before rinsing it off. A plastic colander is useful for this purpose (see right). Only rinse the gravel in small batches; this makes it easier to wash it thoroughly, removing all traces of disinfectant. Once the water emerging runs clear, the gravel should be ready to landscape onto the aquarium floor.

Rinse gravel in small amounts at a time: half-fill a colander with it, then rinse under a running tap, stirring it constantly by hand until the water is clear.

SAND

Certain types of fish tend to root in the substrate as part of their natural behaviour, in which case a softer, finer medium than gravel is preferable, at least for part of the area. For example, the elephant-nosed fish (*Gnathonemus* species) likes to search for food on the bottom with its soft, sensitive snout, and a coarse material makes it hard for them to do this. The obvious alternative to gravel is sand, but this tends to impede an undergravel filter; silver sand is preferable, which is less prone to clogging. Ideally, you should use a different method of filtration with a sand substrate. For fish that like soft water, peat may be a better medium than sand (see right).

If you are using sand, you should disinfect and wash it thoroughly before adding it the aquarium, in the same way as for gravel, above. Use a large sieve with a reasonably fine mesh for rinsing rather than a colander, or you may lose most of it down the drain!

white gravel

pearlized gravel

PEAT BASES

For certain fish, such as some killifish, a soft peat base is preferable to gravel, particularly if you want to encourage them to breed. The killifish will burrow into it, most of all when they mate and lay their eggs. Obtain suitable peat from a specialist aquarium outlet; don't be tempted to use the kind of peat sold for garden use. Place the peat in the base, position plants, wood, or stones to help keep it in place, then add the water. At first, some peat will probably float to the surface, but before long it should become saturated and sink again.

At this stage, the water level may be topped up as necessary. A fairly gentle filtration system is usually required in conjunction with this type of substrate, rather than a power or undergravel system.

WARNING

In aquatic stores, you will probably see gravel that has been dyed in various shades, including yellow, red, and blue, but it is best avoided. This is principally because some of the dye might leach out, colouring the water as a result even if it is not harmful to the fish. This type of gravel may also detract significantly from the colour and markings of the fish. Red gravel especially, even of a different shade from the fish, is very dominant, tending to mask brightly coloured fish such as red platies and swordtails.

Plants

Including plants in your aquarium is not just a matter of making it more decorative; aquatic vegetation plays a key role in helping to maintain a well-balanced environment with good water conditions. As with any of the core elements in the aquarium, the planting scheme needs to be carefully planned if it is to be successful. Bear in mind that, just as when gardening on dry land, it will take time for the plants to become established in a new set-up. In some circumstances, living plants are not recommended, however, and you may decide to incorporate plastic substitutes instead.

WHY HAVE LIVING PLANTS?

Real, living plants are almost the lungs of the aquarium; without them, management of the environmental balance may prove more problematic. Plants help to oxygenate the water, which is of vital benefit to the fish. During the hours of daylight, plants convert the carbon dioxide produced by the fish to oxygen; if you look carefully, you may notice streams of tiny bubbles of gas rising from the leaves to the surface.

This conversion of gas forms part of photosynthesis, the process that enables plants to make their own food, using the energy of sunlight, and creates oxygen as a by-product. During the hours of darkness, however, both plants and

The nitrogen cycle and photosynthesis: ammonia from fish waste and organic debris is broken down into nitrate by bacteria. Plants use this nitrate as fertilizer, helping to keep levels down. They also convert carbon dioxide into oxygen during the day, improving the water oxygen levels for the fish.

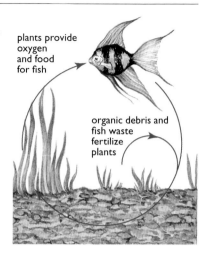

plants provide oxygen and food for fish

organic debris and fish waste fertilize plants

fish use up the oxygen for respiration, releasing carbon dioxide back into the water.

Illumination is therefore vital for aquarium plants, since if they are kept in relative darkness, they will die and water quality will also deteriorate. Never place an aquarium in strong sunlight, but make sure that the lighting is of the correct wavelength, approximating to that of natural light (see pages 66–7); obviously, with plastic plants, lighting is of no direct significance.

Including a variety of plants not only helps to enhance the overall appearance of the aquarium – it also improves water quality, provides retreats for nervous fish, and creates surroundings that more closely echo the fish's natural habitat.

dwarf crypt

twisted vallisneria

Cryptocoryne wendtii

dwarf hygrophilia

The nitrogen cycle

The other key role played by plants is in the nitrogen cycle (see left). The fish's waste, in the form of ammonia, is broken down by beneficial bacteria first to less toxic nitrite and then to nitrate. High nitrate levels are not recommended, particularly in aquaria for fish that naturally inhabit flowing rather than relatively stagnant stretches of water. Aquatic plants help to lower the level of nitrate, by using it as a fertilizer to assist growth.

In aquaria without living plants, it is more important to make regular partial water changes to dilute the nitrate level. In addition, there is more likely to be a problem with excess algae, microscopic plants that may be present in the water or introduced with new fish. Algae multiply very rapidly, often spreading onto the glass as well as decor in the aquarium, including the leaves of plastic plants, since they face no competition for the nutrients dissolved in the water.

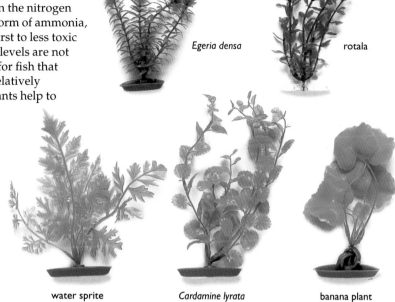

Egeria densa rotala

water sprite *Cardamine lyrata* banana plant

If your tank includes fish that tend to eat or damage real plants, you may have to substitute artificial plants instead. These come in anchoring troughs to weigh them down in the substrate.

PLANNING A PLANTING SCHEME

If you intend including real plants in your aquarium, then you must consider the substrate carefully, because this is where most of the plants will be placed. Although aquatic plants absorb nutrients through their leaves rather than via their roots, a suitable substrate can encourage healthy root growth. You may obtain special baked clay gravel containing trace elements for this purpose, although ordinary gravel is generally suitable.

It is a good idea to draw up a rough planting guide for the aquarium at the outset, which also incorporates other features such as rockwork and bogwood. When buying plants, check their potential eventual size; some aquarium plants can start to dominate a tank if the conditions are ideal for them. Another option is to buy a group of plants specially intended for an aquarium of a

particular size; these collections are also often better value than buying several plants individually.

A large, upright plant should make a good centrepiece, while other bushier plants of similar size can be placed at the back and around the sides; these help to soften the rigid shape of the tank and also afford hiding-places for fish. It is usual to space out smaller plants (no more than about 10cm/4in tall) around the foreground, making sure that there is plenty of clear space so you can see the fish properly. You can also encourage some plants such as Java fern (*Microsorium pteropus*) to grow on decor in the aquarium, softening the outline of rockwork for example, and helping to create a more natural appearance.

Floating plants

If you are housing any fish that prefer low lighting, include some floating plants at the surface to diffuse the light. These plants also serve to provide a sense of security for the fish, which is particularly important for surface-dwelling species; they instinctively avoid predators by seeking out the spreading leaves of plants for cover to make themselves less visible.

ARTIFICIAL PLANTS

Today's replicas are very realistic in appearance and can be used in aquaria housing species of fish that would otherwise strip living vegetation in their tank or uproot it by their persistent excavation of the substrate.

Choosing the plants

Aquarium plants from various parts of the world are now widely cultivated, but it makes sense to choose those that would normally grow in the same conditions and habitat as your fish. This means that they are more likely to suit the fish and should thrive in the same environment. Make sure any plants you choose will tolerate the conditions in your tank; those that normally grow in soft water are unlikely to thrive in hard water, and few plants will thrive in a lime-based substrate.

Aquatic dealers should have a good selection of plants available. Alternatively, especially if you are looking for an unusual plant, look in fish-keeping journals for advertisements of specialist mail-order suppliers. Bear in mind that seasonal and other factors may still affect supplies at times, so you may need to be patient if you are seeking a specific species.

Buying aquatic plants

The advantage of obtaining plants locally is that you can inspect them before purchase, then take them straight home with you. There is no risk of delays in the mail or chilling during cold weather as may occur when ordering from further afield. Aquatic plants must be kept moist at all times because their foliage is delicate and highly susceptible to drying out.

When selecting plants, only pick those that look healthy and vigorous. Avoid any that are lanky or with abnormally yellow leaves. In general, it is best to buy quite small specimens – they are more likely to settle in well and thrive in new surroundings compared with a large, established plant.

On arrival home, carefully check each plant for signs of invertebrates such as snails or their eggs, usually a jelly-like mass on the underside of the leaves. These might prove to be unwanted visitors because they may start eating the plants. It is also wise to wash the plants in a solution of aquarium disinfectant, to eliminate the risk of introducing any diseases to the tank.

Some plants are sold in small pots, which may generally be left in place; it may even be advantageous to restrict the plants in this way. Left unconfined, their roots will spread freely through the substrate of the tank; if you have an undergravel filter, the roots may well block it, seriously reducing its efficiency.

In any well-planted aquarium, there is a need for regular maintenance, such as thinning and pruning of the plants as well as the removal of dead leaves. Long-handled, stainless steel scissors are ideal for enabling you to carry out these tasks with the minimum of disturbance to the fish.

Amazon sword plants

Some plants make a special feature in their own right – sometimes described as specimen plants. These include members of the *Echinodorus* genus, which are usually known as Amazon sword plants. Originating from the Amazonian region, these plants prefer soft water, and are ideal in a tank housing fish from the same part of the world, such as tetras.

Take care to check on the species on offer, because some species, such as the broad-leaf Amazon sword (*E. bleheri*) may grow to about 40cm (16in), making them too tall for many aquaria. Most *Echinodorus* species have relatively narrow, strap-like leaves, but the spade-leaf plant (*E. cordifolius*) has much broader foliage. The pygmy chain sword plant (*E. tenellus*) is an excellent choice for the front of

When inserting aquatic plants into the substrate, use a planting rod or narrow tool secured to a stick to make a hole without disturbing the fish.

an aquarium, and usually establishes itself readily. It grows to about 7.5cm (3in), but if crowded it tends to grow more upright and so will be slightly taller.

In favourable conditions, *Echinodorus* grow quickly and soon become established. They are also relatively tough plants, and their fronds are not usually the target of excessive damage by fish. You can propagate them quite easily to create new plants: simply split off runners or plantlets that grow off their stems once these reach a reasonable size.

Cryptocorynes

In the wild, where water levels fluctuate through the year, some aquatic plants are only submerged for part of this time, yet in the aquarium they are generally kept consistently under water. In the case of the *Cryptocoryne* genus (often known as crypts) from southeast Asia, this serves to slow the plants' growth, since they develop most rapidly when their leaves are exposed directly to sunlight.

A number of cryptocorynes are potentially too large for the typical aquarium, but the attractive dwarf crypt (*C. nevilii*) is ideal for the foreground, since it should grow no taller than about 10cm (4in).

Cryptocorynes often prefer a finer rooting medium than that used for the aquarium substrate, so it is best to grow these plants in containers. You can then incorporate the most suitable rooting medium

Settle the plant in position, so that its crown is more or less level with the surface of the gravel. Firm it in place using the planting tool, and push the gravel back around it to weight it down and discourage the fish from disturbing the roots.

here for them, without affecting the efficiency of the filtration system. Crypts generally dislike root disturbance in any event, so are best obtained in pots, although you may subsequently divide large plants or split off runners when they are more established.

Sagittarias

Sagittarias are another group that will readily grow out of the water. Members of this genus show a considerable range in size, with the largest species growing over 1m (39in) tall. The dwarf sagittaria (*S. subulata*) is a popular choice for aquaria, being suitable for the mid-ground area of a tank. This grass-like plant can reach a height of 30cm (12in); set it in small groups spaced slightly apart to provide dense cover. The level of illumination can affect its coloration, with dwarf sagittarias often developing a reddish hue when grown in brightly-lit conditions.

Vallisnerias

Tall and elegant, vallisnerias (also known as vallis or eel grass) are a good choice for the mid-region or rear of a tank. The spiralled leaf form, twisted vallisneria (*V. tortifolia*) is often used in the mid-ground, while the taller giant vallisneria (*V. gigantea*), especially the red form, makes a stunning specimen plant at the back of a large aquarium.

Filtration equipment

In an aquarium, fish are obviously kept together at a higher density than they would be in the wild. This inevitably leads to a build-up of their waste which, over a period of time, would be harmful and ultimately even life-threatening to them. The purpose of filtration is to clean the water and assist the natural decomposition of waste (including other organic matter such as uneaten food), so that the fish remain in good health.

UNDERGRAVEL FILTRATION

The most basic filter is the undergravel (UG) type, which fits on the floor of the tank with the substrate gravel on top. This method of filtration is purely biological and relatively low maintenance; unlike with a media filter, there is no need to change any filter wool. Occasionally, the gravel should be stirred to freshen up the filter bed and remove any large particles of detritus that have congregated on the surface.

Numerous holes or slits along the length of the filter allow water to pass through the filter plate, but the filtration process itself actually takes place in the gravel. Here, beneficial aerobic bacteria become established and they act on the fish's waste and any uneaten food, turning it into a nitrate compound. Being aerobic, these bacteria require oxygen, so the substrate itself should be relatively coarse, allowing water containing oxygen as well as the fish's waste, to pass through the filter bed. If the particles are too small, or the bed is very shallow, this will adversely affect the action of this type of filter.

For maximum efficiency, the UG filter should cover the entire base of the tank. The filters are produced in a range of sizes for this reason, but if you have an unusually shaped aquarium, then you can cut the filter to fit accordingly, using a sharp modelling knife.

Normal vs reverse flow systems

With a standard UG filter, the water passes down through the filter bed, being drawn through the base and returned to the tank via the uplift – this is the plastic tube fitting at one corner, powered by an air pump which is left running constantly. These pumps are very inexpensive to operate and the current models are generally quiet in operation.

Some fish-keepers prefer to opt for a reverse flow UG filter, however, which requires an external canister filter as well. This also acts as a pre-filter, with water being drawn out of the aquarium, and passing through

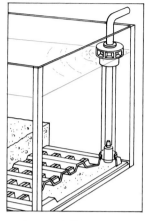

Undergravel filter: water passes through the plate, with bacteria in the gravel.

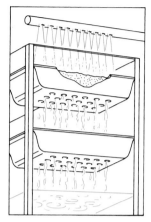

Trickle filter system: the water flow benefits from greater exposure to oxygen.

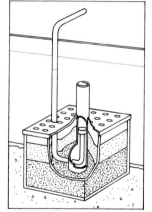

Internal media filter: these tend to be unsightly, but suffice for a small tank.

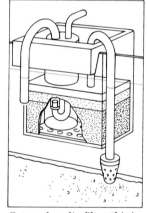

External media filter: this is powerful enough for a large tank, and is easy to maintain.

the canister, before being passed back via the airlift, down into the base of the UG filter. It then moves up through the substrate, which is why this system is described as reverse flow.

The passage of the water via this route helps to prevent any blockage of the filter bed, but it does mean that there is relatively little movement of water at the surface, which is also important to ensure an effective interchange of oxygen and carbon dioxide.

MEDIA FILTERS

Canister filters, unlike the undergravel type, combine biological filtration (from bacteria) with chemical and mechanical filtration. This all takes place within the canister, which contains a filter medium, such as filter wool. This traps particles of dirt within its fibres, while allowing easy passage of the water.

Beneath this wool, there is usually a layer of activated carbon (not to be confused with ordinary charcoal). Its open granules have a very large surface area, so it takes up impurities from the water directly, providing chemical filtration. It also supports a large colony of aerobic bacteria, which act like those in the UG filter bed. Be warned that carbon should not be used in an aquarium containing medication, since it will inactivate the chemicals. Some remedies may also trigger the sudden release of harmful material held in the carbon back into the water.

You will need to change the filter wool regularly so that the filter continues to function effectively. It is worth calculating the cost of filter media in advance, to give you an indication of the likely running costs, which can start to mount up over time. Do not be tempted to economize by using other, non-specialist materials such as cotton wool in place of the filter wool, since these may well be harmful to the fish.

A new set-up

When setting up a new aquarium, bear in mind that biological filtration will take several weeks to be effective, because the bacteria need time to become established. You can speed this process by adding sachets of a compound called zeolite to a canister filter. This natural resin provides a further means of removing ammonia from the aquarium by chemical means, before it can prove harmful. Zeolite sachets can be regenerated easily by immersion in salt water overnight.

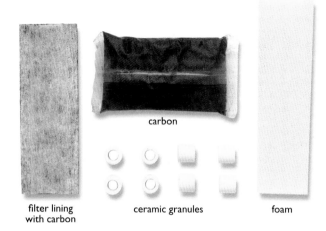

filter lining with carbon   carbon   ceramic granules   foam

Some types of filter media have a large surface area for bacteria to colonize; others include material to remove coarse particles and also incorporate activated carbon.

Filtration through peat

On occasions, especially with fish that require soft water conditions, granulated black peat can be added to the canister filter. The peat is a valuable source of minerals and other compounds as well as humic acid, which lowers the pH; it benefits both fish and plants, and has a mild disinfectant action.

Trickle filters

In this recently developed system of filtration, water drawn from the aquarium trickles down through a series of trays filled with filter media. This raises the oxygen level of the water, improving the efficiency of the aerobic bacteria in the filter beds. It is also quite simple to improve the level of filtration by increasing the number of trays in the stack, but there is a drawback in that they take up a relatively large amount of space.

Internal vs. external filtration

The size of the aquarium, and the number and size of the fish, will obviously influence the size of the filter you need. An internal filter, filled with filter media, is located within the tank, and is generally only suitable for a small set-up. External filters may be free-standing or attach to the side of the aquarium on the outside, and obviously have a larger capacity. In the past, box filters were favoured, driven by an air pump, but today external canister filters or power filters that incorporate their own motors are more widely used.

FOAM CARTRIDGE FILTERS

Foam cartridges filter by both biological and mechanical means. Maintenance is critical if they are to be effective:
• Do not wash the sponge under a running tap because this will harm the beneficial bacteria established on it.
• Instead, wring out the sponge in dechlorinated water or, better still, water removed from the aquarium during a partial water change (see page 80).
• Replacing the cartridge is not recommended because it will take several weeks for bacteria to repopulate it.

Heaters and thermostats

In most aquaria today, combined heaterstats are used in preference to separate heater and thermostat units. This is primarily a matter of convenience and neatness; a heaterstat takes up less space in the tank and needs only a single plug. In a large tank, however, separate units may be required to cope with the greater volume of water, or you may need more than one heaterstat.

WHICH TYPE OF HEATER?

It is important to choose a heater or heaterstat of the right kind and power level for the size of your aquarium. Heaters are typically rated at between 25 and 300 watts in terms of power. How much power you need is partly influenced by external factors, such as whether you will be keeping the tank in a relatively warm room, or if there is likely to be a significant drop in the ambient temperature at night.

As a rough guide, you should allow 100 watts per 100 litres (22 gallons) of water in the tank. Provided that it can maintain the water temperature effectively, a less powerful heater component may be preferable to one with the maximum wattage. This is because – in a heaterstat – the heater almost invariably wears out before the thermostat. If the heater remains operating, rather than continually switching on and off, this should prolong the lifespan of the overall unit. If you do need a powerful heaterstat, however, there is very little difference in the initial outlay, even between a 25W unit and a 300W one from the same range.

There are design factors which may also influence the efficiency of an aquarium heater, such as the material comprising the core of the element. Ceramic is especially good for assisting the transference of heat from the heater to the water, especially when combined with external borosilicate glass tubing, which is a highly efficient conductor of heat.

Other heating options

Most heaterstats are generally of a standard length, but there are also several shorter units on the market; these are suitable for use in small or shallow tanks where the water level may not be deep enough to allow a typical heaterstat to be fully submerged.

Certain species of fish may attack the heaterstat – for example, large piranhas have been known to break the glass or even bite through the wiring – which can have catastrophic consequences. One way of pre-empting this potential problem is to use an external pad heater (see right) or to invest in a combined heaterstat and power filter unit, where the heater is safely located in the canister of the filter.

This kind of unit has two further advantages: one is that it takes up less space, and the second, significant benefit is that the heated water is distributed more efficiently around the aquarium, thanks to the output from the filter. Unfortunately, these combined heaterstat and power filters are relatively expensive, compared with the cost of purchasing individual components.

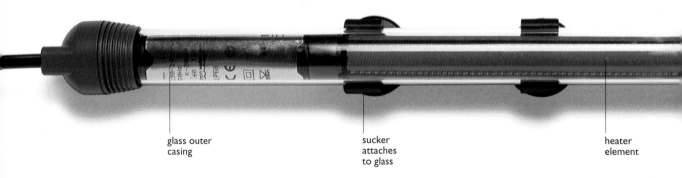

glass outer
casing

sucker
attaches
to glass

heater
element

heater

Heaters come in a range of designs and watt levels, but combined heaterstats are generally preferred nowadays. A separate thermostat is necessary if you are using a heater pad, however. Before removing a heaterstat from the water, always switch it off first and leave it to cool for a few moments.

Pad heaters and thermostats

Another heating option is to use a special heating pad which is fitted externally, either at the back of the aquarium or beneath it – ideal if you are keeping aggressive fish. These thin, flexible heating pads are manufactured in a range of sizes. They may also be useful if you need to lower the water level in the tank, as when breeding substrate-spawning killifish; in these circumstances, it would be difficult to incorporate a conventional heaterstat. A heating pad's output needs to be controlled by a separate thermostat. An external type, which fits outside the aquarium, may prove to be more flexible than an internal thermostat, although it must not be exposed to the water.

THERMOSTATS

Most modern thermostats are based on solid state electronics (with no moving parts), and consist of a control unit, linked to a variable heat switch and a temperature sensor in a circuit board. Once the required temperature is set via the heat switch, this registers in the control unit, and the sensor detects the actual water temperature. As the water cools, this information is transmitted back to the control unit, activating the heater. Once the heater raises the water temperature to the predetermined level, the control unit switches off the heater again.

When buying a heaterstat or thermostat, make sure that it can be easily adjusted, although many units are pre-set during manufacture to about 25°C (77°F), which is ideal for most tropical aquaria. You can check on the calibration and whether the unit is working correctly by placing the heaterstat in a bowl of water and testing the water temperature after 30 minutes with a reliable in-tank thermometer. Once set, it should not normally need to be adjusted again, although there may be occasions, with sick fish for example, when raising the temperature slightly may well be beneficial.

Solid state thermostats are generally more responsive and maintain the water temperature at the preset level more accurately than traditional thermostats based on a bimetallic strip (see below). Most units can be used safely for at least three years.

Bimetallic thermostats

The potential risk of failure in the case of a bimetallic thermostat is inherent in its design. This type of unit includes two strips of metal, one of which is copper, that are fixed together. The two types of metal have different rates of expansion and contraction, so when they reach the preset temperature, the heat makes the strip bend upwards, activating a relay switch which in turn switches off the power to the heater. As the metal cools, so this contact is lost, and power is restored to turn on the heater again.

Over time, these movements are likely to become less reliable and corrosion may also occur. This carries the serious danger that the thermostat might no longer act to turn the heater off, allowing the water temperature to keep rising, which would soon be fatal for the fish. As a precaution against this, you could include an aquarium alarm, which will give an audible signal in the event of a sudden shift in temperature.

element bedded in base

WARNING

When selecting a heaterstat, look for a model where the power is switched off automatically if the unit accidentally becomes exposed above the water level. Without this important safety feature, the glass casing could shatter in such an eventuality.

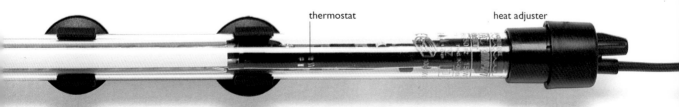

thermostat   heat adjuster

Water conditions: pH

Water is as vital to fish as air is to us, but fish kept in an aquarium are in an enclosed environment, so are entirely reliant on you to provide them with the water conditions they need. Fish have varying water requirements: some need acidic water, others neutral or alkaline water. Unfortunately, you cannot tell just by looking at water whether it is suitable for your fish.

The chemical constituents present in tap water vary, depending on its source. Water that has filtered down through chalk, for example, before going into the supply system, has a different chemistry from that of rain water that has fallen into a pond. There are two principal aspects of water chemistry that are important in an aquarium – the pH value (how acid or alkaline it is) and its degree of hardness (see pages 58–9).

The pH scale

Water may be acidic, neutral, or alkaline, and this is measured in terms of its pH (see diagram, below). Water is defined chemically as H_2O, which indicates that it is composed of hydroxyl (OH) and hydrogen ions (H). The pH reading reflects the relative proportions of these ions. Where hydrogen ions predominate, the water is acidic, whereas an excess of hydroxyl ions results in alkaline water. At pH7 (neutral), the hydrogen and hydroxyl ions are evenly balanced. As this figure decreases, the water becomes more acidic, whereas if it rises, the water sample turns increasingly alkaline.

The pH scale is logarithmic, which means that a change of just one unit actually reflects a tenfold alteration in the concentration of the ions. For fish, this would be a dramatic shift. Most species live within a pH range of 5-9.5, with the specific figure remaining relatively constant under normal circumstances.

The pH scale runs from 0 to 14, with pH7 being neutral. Below pH7 is acid (the lower the number, the more acidic it is); above pH7 is alkaline (the higher the number, the more alkaline it is).

How fish adapt

Water chemistry influences the fish's own internal body chemistry, which can adapt, partly owing to a hormone in the blood and the gill membranes. If the pH of the fish's blood starts to fall, bicarbonate ions are used to maintain the correct level. Conversely, if it starts to rise, then these ions are removed from the fish's circulation.

If the change is too great for the fish to adjust, however, then they will start to sicken; this is why it is so important to monitor the pH of the aquarium water regularly. You can do this quite easily with a test kit (see far right) or a pH meter, which has a probe that you dip into the water sample to test it.

ADJUSTING THE pH

If you need to make an adjustment to the pH of the water, do it gradually, so that the fish are not subjected to dramatic changes in their environment.

Alkaline water

To maintain alkaline conditions, you can add calciferous material to the tank; its impact will decline over time so you will need to replace it periodically. Water naturally contains substances that act as buffers, helping to prevent an increase in acidity, but you can also buy buffering agents for this purpose. Using a substrate that contains limestone is suitable where alkaline water is required.

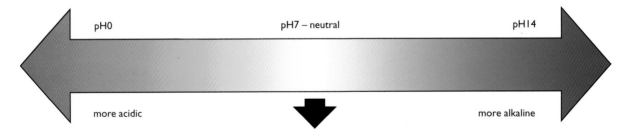

pH0   pH7 – neutral   pH14

more acidic   more alkaline

Acidic water

Where more acidic conditions are required, the simplest method is to add aquarium peat to the filter, if you are using a canister-type flow unit rather than an undergravel system. For maximum effect, you should replace this peat regularly – probably every three weeks or so. It will be easier to achieve the desired effect where the water is naturally soft, since this the relatively high levels of dissolved bicarbonate and similar chemicals that have a buffering effect.

Maintaining the desired acidic pH level in hard water is more difficult and you will need to take additional steps, simply because there is a much greater risk of fluctuations under these conditions. Adequate aeration of the water is especially important, to remove carbon dioxide, which would otherwise cause the pH to fall too low. Partial water changes are also vital; these will help to counter the excess increase in acidity which results from biological filtration, caused by the production of nitric acid (see below).

Proprietary test kits provide a cheap and simple means of testing water, although they may be difficult to use if you are colour blind. A pH test meter is an alternative option. If using a kit, follow the instructions, and add the reagent to the water sample.

Partial water changes

Changing a proportion of the water regularly is a crucial part of basic aquarium maintenance, helping to keep the water clean and remove some of the fish's waste without disturbing the fish. Water changes help to dilute the level of acidity, preventing the pH from falling too low. The volume of water removed depends on the individual tank, but as a guide, you should aim to replace 20–25 percent of the water, every three or four weeks. Check the pH afterwards to determine the effect of the water change and adjust the volume accordingly if necessary in the future. Similarly, regular monitoring will help you decide when to carry out the change.

Put the lid on the tube, shake it, then wait the recommended period of time before comparing the colour of the liquid in the tube with that on the chart.

pH and filtration

Water that is excessively acidic will adversely affect the functioning of a biological filter, since the aerobic bacteria that populate it prefer a neutral pH. If this figure falls below pH6, their level of activity will be seriously compromised. This, in turn, could have a serious effect on the overall water quality, which must be addressed quickly or the fish will suffer.

As well as partial water changes (see above), adding zeolite sachets to a canister filter will lessen reliance on biological filtration, because this compound removes ammonia directly (see page 53), by chemical means. In an acidic, soft water aquarium, it is preferable to use a filter of this type, rather than a simple power filter that depends almost entirely on biological activity.

WARNING SIGNS

Although you should avoid most problems with shifts in pH by good preparation followed by regular maintenance and monitoring of the water, you should also stay alert for warning signs in the fish themselves. For example, if fish are suddenly transferred to unsuitable water conditions, then they usually become hyperexcitable, swimming around wildly and displaying difficulty in breathing. If the cause of the problem is not detected, they will die soon afterwards.

Where there is a more prolonged build-up of acidity, then you may notice excess mucus on the sides of the fish's body, with the skin assuming a reddish tone, although this is sometimes indicative of bacterial infection. Similar behavioural signs occur in excessively alkaline conditions. Fish suffer alkalosis, with erosion of the fins and increased difficulty in breathing.

Water conditions: hard or soft?

You probably know whether the tap water in your area is naturally hard or soft by certain tell-tale signs: in a soft-water area, soap typically lathers well, while in a hard-water region, you will notice that your kettle and shower-head need regular descaling. As with the pH, the degree of hardness in the water has a much greater impact on fish than it does on us, and you need to provide your collection with appropriate conditions.

Different fish species have differing needs in terms of water quality. Most tropical aquarium fish thrive in soft water surroundings, such as species from the Amazon basin, where the rivers are fed directly by rainfall. Some fish require hard water, however, such as the Rift Valley cichlids. The water in the lakes of the Rift Valley, as elsewhere, reflects the underlying chemistry of the rocks in which they formed. Obviously, you will not be able to alter the relative hardness of your water supply at source, but you may need to adjust it to meet the requirements of your fish.

Water chemistry may be greatly affected by the natural rocks in the area where it occurs. In limestone areas, such as these limestone caves, the water is invariably hard.

WATER HARDNESS
The relative hardness of water reflects the amount of dissolved salts present in it. Rainwater falling from the clouds is soft – and pure, in the sense that it has not been in contact with rock. If water filters down over limestone, however, then it acquires ions which dissolve in it, making it harder. In general, the nearer the water is to its natural source, the softer it should be, although water that has travelled over impervious rock, such as granite, may remain relatively soft.

Temporary and permanent hardness
There are two sub-divisions of general or total hardness, often abbreviated to GH. One part is temporary hardness, which can be removed by simply boiling the water. It results from calcium and magnesium bicarbonate, responsible for those whitish 'fur' deposits in kettles in hard-water areas. The remaining part – permanent hardness – is primarily from calcium sulphate; it cannot be removed by boiling the water.

For the aquarium, the temporary fraction is of most significance, since the bicarbonates serve as a buffer and so help to maintain the pH as explained previously.

TO BOIL OR NOT TO BOIL?

Some aquarists opt to soften the water in the aquarium by boiling it, but this is not entirely satisfactory. It may take a long time to boil, and then cool, enough water to fill an aquarium. In addition, boiling only lowers the level of temporary hardness and the chemical change will gradually be reversed, because of carbon dioxide in the water.

Unfortunately, there is no single universal scale used to measure hardness, and this can give rise to confusion. The simplest system is that which uses the number of milligrammes of calcium carbonate in a litre of water. In order to convert to the °DH scale, this figure has to be multiplied by 17.9.

There are test kits available so you can check your tap water quite easily, to gain an accurate indication of its relative hardness, and you can measure both temporary and permanent hardness separately.

Dilution

One simple way of softening the water is to dilute the required volume of hard water with a safe source of soft water. Unfortunately, rainwater – once the obvious natural choice – is no longer reliably safe since it may contain pollutants, which could harm the fish. Distilled water, often stocked in grocery stores, is a better option.

By testing the relative hardness of the two water sources, you can achieve the required level of hardness by means of the following equation:

• Relative hardness (mg/litre of calcium carbonate) = (volume in litres x hardness of hard water) + (volume in litres x hardness of soft water), divided by the total volume of water.

Ion exchange

Another common means of softening water for an aquarium is to use an ion exchange resin produced for this purpose. As its name suggests, this swaps ions, effectively reducing the level of calcium (which makes water hard). Make sure it substitutes hydrogen ions for calcium; many ion exchange systems utilize sodium rather than hydrogen for this purpose, which leads to an undesirable and dramatic increase in the pH.

The resin will become saturated after a while, and should be treated to reactivate it. Run off and discard the first initial output from the ion exchange resin in all cases, because it may contain toxic chemicals in the form of amines.

Trace elements

Using an ion exchange resin results in the presence of carbonic acid and carbon dioxide. The former reduces the pH in the aquarium, but effective aeration removes the excess carbon dioxide quite rapidly. More significant are the trace elements, which are needed in small amounts for the fish's health. This is why pure distilled water or rainwater alone is not ideal; it should be mixed with ordinary tap water, which contains trace elements.

Other means of water softening

A system called reverse osmosis is sometimes used, which is certainly effective but also costly. Other methods work less well, but simply adding peat to a canister filter serves to soften the water to some degree (see page 57), by absorbing the calcium molecules. Certain aquarium plants can also affect the water chemistry, by making use of the dissolved calcium for their growth. Unfortunately, the effects are not entirely dependable. The lesser duckweed (*Lemna minor*), which grows well in a tropical aquarium on the water surface, is one of the most effective plants for this purpose. You may need to curtail its growth periodically, because it can mask the entire surface of the water if its spread is not kept in check by the fish. Other coldwater duckweeds have a similar effect on water chemistry, but they will not thrive in such a heated environment.

The table below indicates the water conditions different fish groups need. If your local water conditions are not suitable for the fish you intend to keep, you will have to adjust them.

WATER TYPE	FISH GROUPS
FRESHWATER very soft 0–6° DH	Characins, barbs, killifish, discus
soft/medium-hard 7–15° DH	Catfish, loaches, goldfish, most cichlids, gouramis
hard 15° DH	African Lake cichlids, livebearers, Australian rainbowfish
BRACKISH 1 tsp salt/ 5 litres plus	*Monodactylus*, mollies, Australian rainbowfish
MARINE S.G. 1.023	All tropical and coldwater saltwater fish, invertebrates

Siting your aquarium

When it comes to choosing the location for your aquarium, take the time to think ahead and consider all the relevant factors so that you get it right. It may seem obvious, but it is very important to site the tank correctly at the outset. If it is in a poor position, you will end up having to empty the tank, transferring the fish elsewhere on a temporary basis, and starting again, because of the weight of the water and decor in the aquarium. This is not only immensely time-consuming, but it would also be stressful for the fish.

Sunlight

It may be tempting to have the aquarium in good natural light, but you must avoid placing it in front of a window. Sunlight streaming in through the glass is bound to affect the water temperature, and on hot days, it may even make it rise to levels that would be fatal for the fish. Another problem is that, as the water temperature increases, it cannot hold as much dissolved oxygen. This leaves the fish vulnerable, not only to excessively warm water, but also to a potential shortage of oxygen if their aquarium becomes too hot.

The ideal position for an aquarium is usually against a wall, and possibly even in the corner of a room. This will help nervous fish to settle down without fear of being approached from all sides, although if you have made sure that there is sufficient cover for such species within the tank, they should soon settle down and will not swim around wildly for long.

Siting the tank against a wall also means that you can use a printed background scene to good effect, since only the picture on the front will be visible. These backgrounds depict a range of appropriate natural scenes, and are available to fit tanks of various sizes or may usually be trimmed if necessary.

The design of the room

The best location for the tank depends on the layout of the room, since clearly much of the enjoyment of having an aquarium will be derived from watching the fish, aside from the possibility of breeding them.

- It is best not to place an armchair directly in front of the aquarium, simply because this will block access, which will be essential for feeding the fish and maintaining the tank.
- A clear area is preferable, not next to a door – the vibrations as this is opened and shut will be transmitted into the tank and could upset the fish, especially at first.
- For the same reason, it is not a good idea to select a site near a television or stereo system. There is also a risk that any water spillage will damage electrical equipment, so do not place a CD system, for example, on a rack beneath a tank.
- Avoid placing any lamps right next to the aquarium, partly in case of accidental water spillage, and also because bright light could prove to be disturbing for certain catfish and other species that are relatively nocturnal in their habits and become active under low lighting conditions.

A number of factors need to be considered before you decide on the site for your aquarium. It is worth working it out carefully in advance, or you may have to empty the tank to move it.

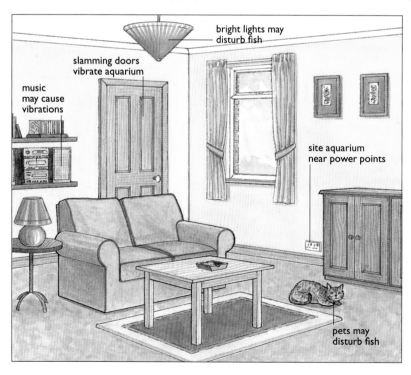

bright lights may disturb fish

slamming doors vibrate aquarium

music may cause vibrations

site aquarium near power points

pets may disturb fish

This all-in-one aquarium is a typical starter kit, with all the components in place in an acrylic tank. Although relatively small, it would still be too heavy to lift safely once full, so correct siting is of prime importance.

(230lb) once it is full of water – that's roughly equivalent to six big sacks of potatoes, so you can see why you should never attempt to shift a full tank.

If there is space in your room, and your budget will allow, you may decide to buy a special, purpose-designed cabinet for the aquarium. These are produced in a variety of styles and designs, often incorporating a cupboard area beneath the tank itself to house supplies such as food. Unlike standard furniture, these cabinets are reinforced to take the weight of the full tank without bowing.

A cheaper option is a metal stand, which is also built to support the tank at a convenient height so that you can attend to the needs of the fish without difficulty. Some stands even accommodate two tanks, but this is not always convenient when it comes to servicing the lower aquarium. In terms of positioning this type of stand, first ensure that the floor area is absolutely level, using a spirit level; if necessary, make any adjustments before setting the tank in position with secure wooden blocks under the feet. Any discrepancy at the base will be reflected in the water level once the aquarium is full, placing greater stress on the glass.

The power supply

Another key aspect to bear in mind when deciding where your aquarium should be sited is the location and accessibility of a power point for the various leads. Try to select a site that will allow you to connect the electrics easily, bearing in mind that the heaterstat (or the heater and thermostat if you have separate units), the filter and air pump, plus the lights will all require an electrical supply.

For safety's sake, it is not sensible to have wirestrailing over the floor, especially if you have young children or pets. As an extra precaution, you may want to tape the plug and the switch in position, and add a label advising people not to switch off the power (see also warning box, below right).

Do not overload the power point with plugs fitted into an adaptor. It is safer to connect the leads into a junction box, in the form of a cable tidy, even if you have to remove the plugs. Alternatively, use a multi-socket connector, with the correct number of spaces for plugs, and a single outlet running to the socket; this will also be fused for safety. This saves the need to rewire any equipment, solves the problem of trailing wires, and provides extra cable so the aquarium may be moved further from the power point if necessary.

Support for the aquarium

A secure base is essential for the tank, because a typical aquarium, measuring 90cm long x 30cm wide x 38cm high (36in x 12in x 15in) will weigh in at roughly 104kg

---

WARNING

When choosing a socket for your aquarium equipment, remember that this must be left switched on constantly. If accidentally disconnected, the fish will be left without heat and filtration, which could prove fatal if not detected at an early stage (see also 'Coping in a power crisis', page 108). If possible, choose a part of the room where there is effectively a spare socket. If you use one that forms part of a double socket, you can protect the aquarium switch with a commercial plastic clip. This will ensure that the aquarium power point is not turned off by mistake when the other socket is used.

Setting up the aquarium

Although you may well want to rush out and choose the fish for your aquarium, the correct approach is to set up the tank first, and get the water conditions right, before you obtain any fish. If you buy the fish first, they are likely to become chilled while waiting for their new home to be prepared. In addition, if there are any unexpected hitches, such as a failure in the heating system for example, this could create serious problems, because you would need to find a replacement urgently.

PREPARING THE TANK

The first step is to wash or hose down the tank, and check it carefully all over for signs of damage. With frameless tanks, the base sheet of glass has sometimes become compressed and broken at a corner, for example. For this reason, you should never stand a tank up on its edge, but keep it off the ground while emptying it.

Rinsing the tank should also wash out any minute particles of glass that might remain after the sheets were cut. These could possibly injure the fish, especially if they become lodged in the gills.

Placing the tank

The next stage is to stand the tank on a layer of expanded polystyrene, which will absorb any unevenness in the surface. Without this precaution, the tank might start to leak once full, because of the greatly increased water pressure on the vulnerable part of the tank.

The filter plate

If using an undergravel filter, you should then fit the filter plate, ensuring that it lies flat on the base of the tank with no gaps. The gravel should be washed, disinfected, rinsed, and drained, then tipped carefully on top, and spread out to the appropriate depth.

When setting up an aquarium, wipe out the inside carefully, particularly in a glass tank. Treat second-hand tanks with an aquarium disinfectant.

PREPARING THE DECOR

Once the substrate is in place, you can add the tank decor in the form of real or replica rocks or wood. Take care to leave a relatively clear space at the front of the aquarium, and do not cover too much of the base in all, because it impedes areas of the undergravel filter, so reducing its efficiency.

If you decide to use natural rocks, rather than lightweight substitutes, it is usually safest to obtain them from an aquatic store to ensure that they are safe for aquarium use. Use only impervious rocks such as granite or slate, which will not dissolve and affect the water chemistry. Limestone is only suitable for aquaria accommodating fish that require hard water conditions. Should you decide to collect your own rocks, and are unsure if they contain any limestone, you can test them easily. Simply pour some vinegar (acetic acid) over

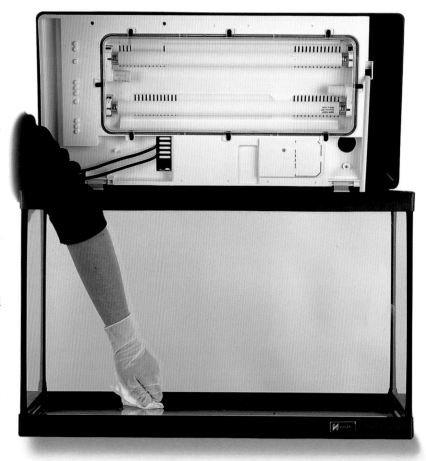

them outside. If the rock starts to fizz, then this indicates the presence of calcium carbonate (limestone).

All rockwork, irrespective of its origins, should be scrubbed with a clean brush, to remove any mud or contamination. Then treat it with a solution of aquarium disinfectant, rinse it, and place it in the tank, making sure that it is stable and settled in the substrate.

Clay flowerpots

Clay pots are a useful addition to the aquarium, and have a number of advantages over rockwork. Only a relatively small proportion of their surface area is in contact with the gravel bed, so the effects on an undergravel filter are minimal. Roughly broken in half, a flowerpot provides a valuable retreat for certain fish, such as catfish, and may also be used for spawning by a number of species. The best way to break a pot without smashing it to pieces is to crack it carefully with a chisel.

Bogwood

Artificial wood is easier to work with than natural bogwood, partly because it will not float – real wood floats unless it is saturated. Bogwood from aquatic outlets is normally sold in a dry state; it takes several weeks to be fully saturated so must be wedged into place when you first position it.

Boil or at least soak the bogwood several times, using fresh water each time. This prevents it from leaching and discolouring the water, as well as clearing it of any pathogens which might harm the fish. Another option is to saturate the wood, then varnish it. This is also not without its problems, however: you must wait for the varnish to dry completely, and it is usually recommended to use more than one coat to ensure that the wood is totally sealed. There is also a risk that fish may nibble at the varnish, particularly if it has bubbled at any point, and they could become poisoned.

Tip in the washed gravel, then spread it evenly over the base. Add slightly more at the back, sloping down to the front.

> ### WARNING
>
> Never pile up rocks, even small ones, in the aquarium; if they were to collapse, they might not only injure a fish, but could also crack the glass. The risk of collapse is most likely with large fish that dig in the substrate, such as certain cichlids, however, inadvertently altering the current from a filter could also have the same result. If you want to slant a piece of slate, for example, use silicone sealant to anchor it firmly in place onto another piece of rock beforehand, rather than leaving it loosely supported.

Wood is a good anchorage point for some aquatic plants, such as Java fern (*Microsorium pteropus*), adding to the natural landscape effect in the aquarium. It is also important for the well-being of some suckermouth catfish (of the family Loricariidae); if you keep these fish, supply them with some untreated bogwood.

Planting and filling the tank

Once the aquarium is in position, and you have checked that it is correctly level and prepared the substrate and decor, you can move on to the next stage. The easiest way to proceed is to partly fill the tank, then position the plants and make any other adjustments, before you finish filling the tank with water. If you are using an external pad heater, place it beneath the tank before filling, or attach it to the back at a later stage.

Adding the heaterstat

First check that any rocks are in position and supported before adding the heaterstat, otherwise it could be damaged accidentally. Heaterstats are supplied with rubber suckers which need to be moistened so that they fix to the side of the tank. Locate the supports so that they do not fit directly round the heating element within the glass tube. Arrange the suckers so that they hold the unit firmly to the glass, taking care not to alter the calibration of the thermostat. Never switch on this kind of unit until the tank has been filled with water.

Set a saucer on top of the gravel so as not to disturb it when you pour in the water. Check the water temperature at this stage, to ensure that it is at a suitable level for the plants.

If you need more than one heaterstat, space them evenly around the tank to ensure good heat distribution. Set the unit or units horizontally rather than vertically, otherwise the heated water will rise up directly past the thermostat, switching it off prematurely.

Certain types of fish may lay their eggs on the heater, but you can prevent this by encircling it with a tube of plastic mesh, without inhibiting the circulation of water. Do not allow this protective cover to come into direct contact with the heater, and fix it in such a way that you can easily slide it off for cleaning.

Filling the aquarium

To fill the tank, the ideal container is a plastic watering can, with a graduated scale. This is useful for calculating how much water conditioner to add, removing harmful chlorine or chloramine. When making partial water changes, you must treat the water before adding it to the tank, of course, but initially you can wait until the aquarium is full, because there are no fish in it yet.

Once the tank is about a quarter full, put in the plants. This means they are more likely to stay in position, especially if cuttings, than if planted into the substrate of an empty tank.

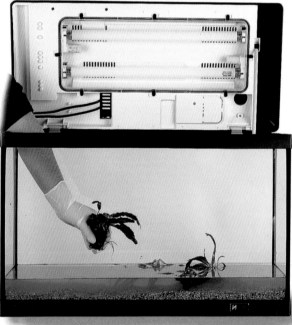

Planting

Add the plants once the tank is about a quarter full. If you are including real plants, make sure that the water temperature is roughly at the level you plan to maintain in the aquarium. Do not let the plants dry out at any stage – if you cannot set them in the tank at once, keep them under water until you are ready. If planting cuttings, keep them in clumps, allowing space between the individual sections for growth; a pencil is a useful tool for preparing holes of the right size.

When positioning potted-up plants, you will need to excavate a larger area of gravel for them, and you may need to bank up the substrate to conceal the pot. Another tip is to position the pot behind rockwork or bogwood to hide it.

Handle the plants as little as possible, to avoid damaging their leaves or stems. If using fertilizer pellets, bury these alongside the plants once they are in position. Put in any floating plants at a later stage, once the aquarium is full.

Air matters

At this point, carry out any other adjustments, such as altering the uplift pipe of the undergravel filter. This may be necessary if you want to fit a powerhead at the top, to ensure better circulation of the water. If the uplift is too tall to accommodate the powerhead, you can cut it down to the right length with a hacksaw.

Fill the tank with water, check all the components are working properly, and make any necessary adjustments. You can then add a water conditioner.

If you are including an airstone or similar device, place it in the tank at this stage, with a multiple 'gang valve' fitted into the tubing line, to protect the air pump.

Filters and filling

If using an internal power filter, fit it at this stage, usually at the rear. The water outlet at the top is normally directed along the tank for good water circulation, although it can be angled across the tank if preferred. The unit may be totally submerged, but more often, the actual outlet is positioned level with the water surface.

An external canister filter is not incorporated into the tank, but it is easier to fit the outlet tube now, just above the substrate. The filtered water can then be run back into the tank from above, via a spray bar for example.

Once everything is in place, add the remainder of the water to fill the aquarium to just below the level of the horizontal glass bars at the top. The next stage is to sort out the covering and lighting, before connecting up the electrics and switching on all the equipment.

Hoods and lighting

The combination of electricity and water is clearly a potentially hazardous one, so any electrical equipment you use for the tank must be specifically designed for aquarium use. It is also essential to include a barrier at the top of the tank, where condensation and lighting would otherwise come into contact. This can be achieved by fitting a condensation tray – usually just a sheet of plastic or cover glass supported on the glass shelves about 1cm (1/2in) below the rim. This cover also serves to prevent any fish from leaping out of the water, but a proper hood with a light is equally essential, particularly if the aquarium includes living plants.

Why lighting is necessary

Lighting the aquarium has two main functions. Providing the right sort of light (from the correct part of the spectrum – like natural daylight) enables plants to photosynthesize (see pages 48–9) and maintain healthy water conditions for the fish; without it, the plants will die rapidly, polluting the tank.

Lighting also illuminates the occupants, especially worthwhile for vivid types such as cardinal tetras, adding greatly to overall effect. Special fluorescent strip lights are generally used for most freshwater aquaria since their heat output is minimal and does not disrupt the stability of the water temperature; ordinary fluorescent tubes are unsuitable because the light output is from the wrong part of the spectrum.

For aquarium use, there are special fluorescent tubes which give out light from the right part of the spectrum for plant growth. A reflector directs light down into the water.

fluorescent tube for an aquarium

reflector panel

Correct lighting is essential if the plants are to photosynthesize. In the cycle of photosynthesis, the plants make food for their own growth and release oxygen when the aquarium is lit, which benefits the fish.

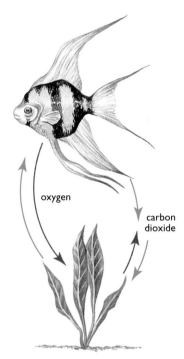

 night

day

oxygen

carbon dioxide

Lighting checkpoints

• Use lighting tubes that are purpose designed for aquaria. They emit light from the red and blue parts of the spectrum, similar to natural sunlight.
• Tubes are sold in a range of lengths. If necessary, depending on the fitments in the hood, you may run two tubes in parallel.
• Remember, the level of illumination needed is partly affected by the location of the tank and its depth. As a guide, allow roughly 10 watts (W) of fluorescent light for every 30cm (12in) of tank length.
• Make sure the lighting runs the whole length of the aquarium, to provide even illumination in the tank.
• It is usually recommended to light the tank for eight to ten hours a day. You can use a timer switch to control them automatically if you prefer, provided that the control unit can operate fluorescent lighting (many timers are for incandescent lights only).
• Beware of overlighting: this tends to trigger excessive algal growth within the aquarium, although this will not be immediately apparent. If you do notice this becoming a problem, one way to counteract it is to reduce the time that the aquarium is lit each day.

Incorporating the lights

At the rear of the hood, there is space to accommodate the light fitments, with the tube itself being fitted between special connectors, which are designed to exclude damp. The pins on the tube serve to anchor it in place here; make sure they do not become bent or otherwise damaged, or the light may not work.

To fit the tube correctly into the hood, anchor it firmly in place using the plastic clips, which should be located close to the ends. Whether the control unit is inside or outside the hood, there should be easy access to the lighting switch. Keep any excess cable tied up in the hood; you might need it, if you move the aquarium to a new position at a later stage.

Subdued lighting

Bright lighting is not always desirable, especially if you want to watch fish that normally live in darkened surroundings. It may be better to opt for plastic plants and a lower wattage output, so as to replicate the light levels in the fish's natural habitat more closely. This applies in the case of blind cave fish (*Astyanax fasciatus mexicanus*), for example, as well as various catfish.

Another means of screening the water and diffusing the light is to incorporate floating plants. In this case, make sure that the tank is not filled up to the maximum level or the plants may come into contact with the condensation tray or cover glass. The water here is almost bound to wedge the plants to some extent, and before long, in spite of the bright light, they may well start to rot. As a precaution, allow a gap of about 15cm (6in) from the rim. The currents in the aquarium tend to wash floating plants into a corner, especially if you use a power filter. Provided that there is an adequate circulation of air, however, they should remain healthy.

WARNING

Do not wait until a fluorescent tube light stops working before you replace it. The output of its beneficial wavelengths of light decreases over a period of time, which in turn means that the benefits to the plants will be correspondingly reduced. As a guide, the normal recommendation is for the tube to be replaced every 10–12 months, although obviously this depends greatly on the length of time the light is switched on each day. Some types of fluorescent lighting also last longer than others, so check the packaging of the tube itself at the time of purchase.

Lighting plants above water

If you are especially interested in aquatic plants, you might consider a more specialist arrangement – certain tropical plants naturally occur close to the water and these may be attached instead to the back of the aquarium, above the water line. This means you necessarily have to allow a much bigger gap between the lights and the water beneath, which also enables aquatic plants that would normally grow up and out of the water to thrive in this kind of set-up.

Unfortunately, this is rarely possible in a typical aquarium, where a relatively large number of fish are housed together, because the reduced volume of water limits the stocking density. If you have the space for a large tank, however, an established aquarium of this type can be immensely striking. You may need an aquarium specially designed for this purpose, and you are also likely to require more powerful lights, for the benefit of any plants that grow actually in the water.

Floating plants diffuse the lighting, and are especially valuable in providing cover for surface-dwelling fish, but be careful that they do not start to rot due to condensation.

Conditioning the water

If you have followed all the necessary stages, and checked that the equipment is functioning properly, your aquarium should now be almost ready to receive fish. A final, vital step is to condition the water to make it suitable for them. This removes harmful chemicals such as chlorine or the more toxic chloramine that are often present in tap water.

The dangers of chlorine and chloramine

Water companies add chlorine to the water supply as a safe disinfectant, but unfortunately, this chemical is toxic to fish, even in minute quantities. Most water supplies have a chlorine level of 0.2 – 0.5mg per litre, but as little as 0.1 mg per litre may be sufficient to harm fish. The good news is that chlorine will naturally diffuse out of solution quite rapidly, especially if the water is aerated: allowing it to stand for about 24 hours after pouring should usually be adequate.

Another agent is sometimes added to the tap water in place of chlorine, which is potentially even more toxic to fish. Called chloramine, this chemical is a combination of chlorine and ammonia, and takes longer to diffuse out of solution. Although a standard dechlorinating agent such as sodium thiosulphate will effectively remove chlorine by binding with it, in the case of chloramine, this action would lead to free ammonia in the water. This is especially dangerous in a new aquarium where the filter bed is not yet fully established. You should therefore use a means of effective chemical filtration as well, to strip out the free ammonia from the water. Zeolite sachets are usually recommended for this purpose.

Check with your water supply company if they are using chlorine or chloramine. Fortunately, some of the newer water conditioners on the market have been developed specifically to overcome the toxic effects of chloramine, rather than chlorine on its own, so make sure you use one of these if necessary.

Effects of chlorine poisoning

The active agent that affects the fish is hypochlorous acid, which is formed from the combination of chlorine and water molecules. Fish exposed to tap water that has not been dechlorinated display obvious signs of distress, swimming around wildly at first, in the hope of avoiding the poison. After this, their colour starts to fade, and they become inactive, often shimmying (see page 101) for a time. Their breathing becomes laboured before they die. Some species, usually those that can breathe atmospheric air directly, are less vulnerable than others. Provided that the cause of their distress is recognized in time, immediately adding a dechlorinator to the water should enable them to recover.

Protective conditioner

Using a water conditioner has an additional benefit: It helps to provide a coating for the fish, reinforcing the natural protective mucus barrier on the surface of their bodies. This natural barrier helps to protect the fish from fungal disease and other infections. It may be accidentally damaged when you catch a fish, so making it more vulnerable to disease. Be especially careful if you ever need to handle a fish directly (which is not recommended), and always wet your hands with the aquarium water first, since the protective mucus is then less likely to come off onto your own skin.

Adding a water conditioner will neutralize harmful chemicals that might otherwise endanger the fish's health. It also helps to provide a protective coating on the surface of their bodies.

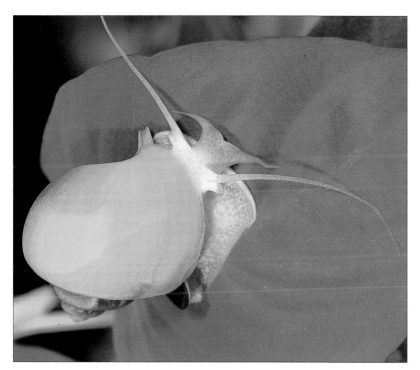

Left: Aquarists differ widely in their views on snails. Apple snails (Ampullaria *species*) *are probably the most widely kept group in tropical aquaria. They grow to a maximum size of about 5cm (2in).*

Below: Snails may prove to be highly prolific, producing large numbers of fertile eggs in a jelly-like mass, which are often laid on the aquarium glass or concealed on the undersides of leaves.

SNAILS

When deciding which species you want to keep, you might consider compatible creatures other than fish, usually invertebrates such as snails. Make sure that your selected species will live in harmony; some fish, such as boxfish for example, readily eat snails. Apple snails (*Ampullaria* species) are a popular choice; these are naturally brownish-green, but there is now a striking bright yellow variant available.

The red ramshorn snail (*Planorbis corneus*) is reddish-brown with a distinctly coiled appearance. They are not entirely vegetarian, so must be excluded from spawning tanks because they will eat the fish eggs.

Feeding snails

Snails browse on algae, helping to keep it in check, but in a new aquarium, where algal growth is minimal, they may well turn their attention to the plants. This can be devastating, especially as the plants are not yet established, so are less able to rejuvenate. It is therefore advisable to add snails only after several months.

Aquatic snails favour certain plants (such as *Hygrophila stricta*), so choose tough, less appetising plants if you plan to include these molluscs. Snails may also eat left-over particles of fish food, but do not rely on them to scavenge and clean up the tank for you.

Breeding snails

The other major problem with snails is their rapid rate of reproduction, especially in the absence of predators. Snails have both male and female sex organs, so having more than one snail invariably gives rise to fertile eggs. The eggs take about three months to hatch, with the young snails being miniature replicas of their parents. Provide additional sources of green food at this stage, to help prevent the growing snail population from eating the plants. At some stage, you will need to curtail their numbers, and this is best achieved by removing at least some of the eggs before they develop. In an aquarium habitat, snails usually live for a couple of years.

FISH AND FROGS

It is not usually wise to mix fish with other vertebrates, especially terrapins, which are highly predatory, but small African dwarf clawed frogs *(Hymenochirus boettgeri)* are sometimes kept alongside them. Choose the tankmates for these amphibians with care, because some fish bite at the frogs' toes. These frogs grow no bigger than about 5cm (2in), so are unlikely to harm fish, except possibly young livebearers. They normally eat whiteworm.

Brackish water

When it comes to setting up an aquarium, the most obvious choice is between a fresh water or a more complex marine set-up, but there is also a third option - a brackish aquarium. Brackish water occurs where sea water and fresh water meet, close to the mouths of rivers and in mangrove swamps. To achieve the right level of salinity, you can use a blend of marine salts available from aquatic stores. Take care to keep the nitrate levels low in this type of aquarium, because brackish water fish are more vulnerable to a build-up of this chemical than most freshwater species.

FISH FOR BRACKISH WATER

Some of the most unusual and interesting aquarium fish have adapted to survive in these conditions, where the salinity may vary widely. Brackish water is suitable for mollies, although they are usually kept in freshwater tanks, which unfortunately makes them more vulnerable to fungal disease and white spot.

Another livebearer that thrives in a brackish tank is the striped four-eyed fish (*Anableps anableps*). Make sure there are no jutting rocks or sharp objects in the aquarium that could damage their vulnerable eyes. The male's gonopodium is directed to one side of the body and he needs to find a female with a compatible genital opening if mating is to succeed. Females have up to four offspring, which are typically 2.5cm (1in) long.

Archer fish

While four-eyed fish are insectivorous, they do not have the hunting capabilities of another brackish water species – the archer fish (*Toxotes jaculator*), which is silver with striking, triangular black markings across its back. It earns its name because of its impressive ability to shoot down insects into the water from overhanging vegetation, spurting droplets of water at them from a short distance away.

Glassfish

Another unusual fish that thrives in brackish water is the Indian glassfish (*Chanda ranga*). Unfortunately, their naturally transparent, glass-like appearance has sometimes been artificially coloured by the unpleasant and cruel practice of injecting them with dyes which show through their bodies. Although most reputable shops refuse to stock dyed glassfish, you may still occasionally see them, but you should never buy any fish in this condition.

Provide a relatively shallow tank for the four-eyed fish (Anableps anableps), with plenty of swimming space – adults may grow up to 30cm (12in) long.

The archer fish (Toxotes jaculator) is fascinating to watch, as it may be persuaded to display its skill, aiming accurately at insects on the sides of the tank above the water level.

The almost transparent glassfish (Chanda ranga) is fairly easy to keep and is best grouped in a small shoal. In its natural state, its coloration is usually pale yellowish-orange to green.

The red tiger scat (Scatophagus argus) *grows to about 15cm (6in) in a tank, and thrives in a small group of around five fish.*

Scats

Certain species of brackish water fish naturally have very variable coloration, such as scats (*Scatophagus argus*). These fish may range in colour from silver to gold or shades of red, while their contrasting darker markings can vary from spots to stripes.

Other fish for a brackish tank

If you are keeping scats, you can provide them with good companions in the form of monos. A shoaling fish by nature, the mono (*Monodactylus argenteus*) has a flattened, silvery body, with yellowish fins, which tend to fade with age. Black stripes run through the eyes and also across its gill covers.

Pufferfish (*Tetraodon fluviatilis*) also thrive in a brackish aquarium, although they may be aggressive and are best kept on their own. While some species inhabit brackish waters, others are adapted to a marine habitat, so check on the exact water conditions needed in advance. Their jaws tend to become overgrown if they do not have enough hard-shelled food, such as river shrimp, and they become unable to eat. In this case, the jaws have to be trimmed under anaesthetic by a vet.

More peaceful by nature is the bumblebee goby (*Brachygobius xanthozona*), which has black and yellow markings and grows to only about 3.5cm (1¹/2in) long. It may be shy, so it appreciates somewhere to hide.

The matter of plants

Most aquatic plants will not grow in salty water, but there are a few that can prove sufficiently adaptable to tolerate a brackish environment. These include the Java fern (*Microsorium pteropus*), which will root on submerged objects such as rocks. Vallisnerias can also

prove sufficiently robust to survive in brackish surroundings but these particular plants will rarely grow as well here as they would in fresh water. The other option is to use plastic plants instead.

Preparing the water

It is quite easy to make up the water for a brackish aquarium, using a suitable marine salts blend from aquarist shops. Treat the water with a dechlorinator before adding the marine salt. This is because dechlorinating chemicals are often less effective in salt water, which could have fatal consequences for the fish. Follow the instructions on the packet for mixing the salt, stirring the recommended quantity of the salt into ordinary tap water, and make sure that it has dissolved completely. Do this in a bucket before you add it to the tank.

Checking salinity

You can measure the salt content of the water quite simply using a hydrometer, available from aquatic stores, which will give you a specific gravity (SG) reading. The water for a brackish tank should have a specific gravity figure of between 1.005 and 1.015. Regular monitoring is vital because as the water evaporates, the remaining water will have a higher concentration.

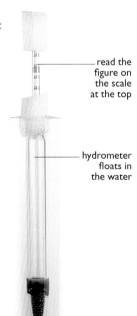

read the figure on the scale at the top

hydrometer floats in the water

Use the hydrometer to take regular readings of the water in the aquarium.

Choosing and caring for fish

Selecting and looking after your fish can be an immensely enjoyable part of fish-keeping. Make sure you give your aquarium a good start: take the trouble to search out and obtain healthy fish, and establish a regular care routine from the outset; this helps you create a well-balanced habitat in which your fish should thrive.

Buying fish

You can buy fish from various sources, ranging from ordinary pet shops to specialist aquatic stores, or even via mail order. The choice partly depends on which types you want. Most pet stores stock a basic range of tropical fish, usually including a selection of livebearers such as guppies, maybe some barbs and similar species, tetras, plus a few of the smaller catfish. These are often quite suitable for a community aquarium, because if the shop only has a few tanks, it will tend to stock popular species that are easy to keep.

On the other hand, if you are seeking specific or more unusual species, you would do better to go to a specialist aquatic store. Check your local business directory for addresses of stores in your area, ask for a recommendation if you already know a fellow enthusiast, or look in the fish-keeping magazines.

CHOOSING A STORE

Once you have decided to set up an aquarium, it is tempting to rush out to buy the fish, but a hasty purchase may soon become a regretted one, so take your time. If you are doubtful about the way in which the fish are kept at one store, or their condition, then err on the side of caution and look elsewhere. The fish themselves are only a relatively small fraction of your investment, compared with the cost of the equipment, but if you don't buy wisely, you could waste both time and money, and land yourself with a lot of frustration and additional problems right from the start.

Also bear in mind that if you add sick fish to the tank, you will endanger the health of their companions as well as any subsequent arrivals. Always aim to start out with the best stock you can find, and keep newcomers in a basic isolation tank at first for this reason, though even this will not guarantee their good health.

Buying locally

There are several advantages to obtaining fish locally where possible. In the first place, they are likely to be acclimatized to the local water conditions, at least to some extent, depending on how long they have been in stock. They will also have only a short journey to their new home, lessening the stress of the move. As a regular customer, you should find it easy to keep a check on any new fish that become available, and you are likely to get better service and a more helpful response in the event of any problems. With a new tank, using a local supplier also makes it more convenient if you want to stock it gradually over a few months.

You can buy both fish and compatible aquatic plants from the same outlet. For more specialist requirements, look for retailers' advertisements in fish-keeping journals.

Store checklist

As with any kind of store, some are better than others. The following tips should help you check if the store is generally a good source for obtaining healthy fish.

Trade membership • Although it is no cast-iron guarantee, look for a store that displays membership of a trade organization. Such bodies run special staff training courses, so in these outlets the staff should be able to offer you sound, knowledgeable advice.

Sick fish • Avoid any store where you spot any dead or diseased fish, even if the species you want look healthy.

Tell-tale tanks • Display tanks often indicate the level of care: check that they are clean and not overcrowded.

Air supply • If the fish are congregating at the surface (not just surface-dwellers) and gasping, they may be suffering from a deficiency of oxygen.

Helpful labelling • Well-labelled aquaria, highlighting the compatibility of the fish and other details such as ease of keeping, as well as prices, usually indicate knowledgeable and responsible management.

Helpful staff • Watching the staff can give a useful insight, particularly their attitude to customers. Are they helpful or off-hand? If you or another customer want a particular pair of fish, but the staff seem unwilling to bother to catch them, trying to fob you off with others, then you may prefer to go elsewhere.

Ordering fish

If you cannot see the species you want, the store may order it specially, particularly if it is a specialist aquatic outlet. They may only do this for a firm order, however, which rather binds you to buying the fish before seeing them, which is not generally recommended. If the

The size of a fish, such as this discus (Symphysodon discus) has a bearing on its cost, with large specimens sometimes being considerably more expensive. Compatible pairs or rarer colours also tend to increase the asking price.

dealer seems knowledgeable and the premises well-run, it may be worth the risk. When seeking breeding stock, this may be more complicated, unless the sexes of the species concerned can be discerned very easily.

Mail order fish

Least satisfactory in general terms, although it works well in many cases, is to buy fish unseen, and have them sent by courier. Shipment is quite costly, so tends only to be used with more expensive fish, often breeding stock. In these circumstances, the breeder or supplier may be prepared to send you photos of the fish they have available before you make your order.

Check when the fish will be dispatched and their likely time of delivery so someone can be at home to receive them. Fish are shipped in insulated packs, so should not be subjected to great variations in water temperature, although shipping may be best delayed if conditions are very cold. Obviously, if there are unexpected delays in transit, this may harm the fish.

EXHIBITION FISH

If you are interested in breeding exhibition stock, then you might need a different approach. It is obviously helpful to visit shows, because this will give you a clear indication of the type of stock that you need, and show you how to display the fish to best effect. This also provides the best way of meeting breeders who may have surplus stock available or be able to recommend good suppliers. Consider joining a specialist society, too – there are organizations representing all the major groups of fish. This will put you in contact with dedicated and experienced enthusiasts, and should give you access to more unusual species that would be hard to obtain from the average aquatic outlet.

Selecting your fish

Once you know which species you want, and have found an outlet that appears to be well-run and carrying healthy stock, you can select your fish. Inspect their condition and spend some time watching them; you should know how the types you want normally look and behave so you can spot problems more easily, and use the points here as a checklist to help you.

Look at all the fish in the tank before deciding. If there are any ailing individuals, hidden among the shoal, this could potentially cause serious problems for your aquarium. A number of diseases are not just spread from fish to fish, but the harmful microbes also survive in the water. Watch the fish as they are being caught, if there any you wish to avoid. It is a good sign if the shop does not have only one net for all the fish, because this may spread disease easily from one tank to another, through contaminated water.

Start small…

It is almost impossible with most tropical fish to be sure of their age, especially if fully grown. Small species such as many livebearers may live for little more than a year, so buying them is something of a lottery. Although less impressive, it is usually better to choose young fish, because it is easier to determine their age.

With larger fish such as oscars (*Astronotus ocellatus*) or some catfish, like suckermouths (*Hypostomus* species), it may still be better to pick smaller individuals. They tend to be considerably cheaper, and more important, often settle down more easily in new surroundings.

A fish's behaviour can give clues as to its health. Some species, such as suckermouth catfish, do not swim around the tank much, so check their fins for fungus, and their overall condition.

This can be especially significant with 'character' fish like oscars which can be taught to feed from your hand.

Furthermore, if you are hoping to breed a pair, this approach can help to prevent aggression, since neither fish will yet be ready to spawn, and the male will not start to bully the female in unfamiliar surroundings. There should then be a greater chance of their being compatible in due course.

A CLOSER EXAMINATION

Check the following points to help you avoid accidentally selecting poor or unhealthy specimens.

Swimming signs • Are the fish swimming normally? Any that appear to be having difficulty may be showing signs of dropsy (see page 98) or a swim-bladder disorder, for which there are no real cures.

Barbels • It may be harder to assess the health of species such as catfish, which tend to remain anchored onto a stone, but there are other indicators. Check that the barbels around the mouth are of even length and do not appear to be inflamed, which sometimes happens, particularly if the substrate is dirty. While a change of environment may well lead to an improvement in their condition, the damaged area could still be vulnerable to fungus.

Plumpness • The fish should appear plump, rather than thin, which could indicate a chronic disease, even piscine tuberculosis. It is obviously easier to assess this if there are several fish for comparison.

Eye check • Make sure that the eyes are not cloudy, and that both are present (except for blind cave fish, where no eyes are visible); occasionally, fry develop missing an eye. If one or both eyes are bulging out of there sockets, this may indicate a condition known as 'pop eye' or exophthalmia; do not buy such fish – they often have no realistic likelihood of recovery.

Fin condition

The condition of the fins is important, especially in species that have prominent or elaborate fins. In some cases, you may notice a few small nicks, particularly in the dorsal and caudal fins, although these usually heal in due course. Abnormally closed down or clamped fins are more worrying, indicating general ill-health.

Severe erosion around the edges of all the fins is highly suggestive of either a weakened fish, or poor water conditions. Under these circumstances, fungus may take a hold, although once the fish are transferred to a fresh set-up, where the level of potential pathogens in the water will be lower, they may well recover without giving further cause for concern.

Scale damage

Take a good look at the fish's scales, because a damaged area here can soon become infected and will start to ulcerate. While it may be possible to treat this, it will be time-consuming and potentially costly. Raised scales, held slightly away from the body, are a sign of general illness and are often seen with other symptoms, such as a reluctance to swim. Avoid any fish like this because they are likely to be seriously ill.

Colour change

In some cases, fish may exhibit poor coloration. If all the fish in the tank are less brightly coloured that you would normally expect, it may well be that the lighting is too bright, which tends to make colours look less vivid. If just one or two individuals seem pale, however, they may be sick or being bullied by others in the group.

A pale, washed-out appearance is typically associated with many types of tetra if kept under powerful lights. In the wild, these fish tend to inhabit areas of water where the level of illumination is relatively subdued; if housed under such conditions, with cover from floating plants, their coloration will very quickly become more vibrant again.

Healthy appetite

If you want to have a final check on the condition of the fish, ask to see them feeding. A fish that is eating well will usually be quite healthy. Unfortunately, some shyer species such as certain catfish may not be ready to eat in this way. With these fish, look in the water for pieces of food such as cucumber, which show signs of having been rasped by the fish's mouthparts – then you can be fairly sure that they are eating properly.

AVOIDING INFECTION

When selecting fish for purchase, if there are obvious signs of a problem such as white spot (see page 104) on some of them, you would do better to shop elsewhere. As well as a possible risk of introducing the infection to the aquarium via water from the tank, even if the fish you choose seem healthy, there is still a risk that they could develop the infection, especially after being transferred to new surroundings. The last thing you want when setting up a new aquarium is to start by medicating the water, particularly if you are faced with a disease that can lie dormant then flare up again in the future.

Settling in

Give your fish a good start in their new home by taking care to transport and settle them in correctly. Once you have made your choice, the fish will be caught and bagged with water for you to take home. Although most reputable aquatic stores do isolate their fish at first, there is unfortunately no guarantee that they will not introduce disease to the aquarium. It is therefore a good idea to have a spare tank for isolating the new fish.

Transporting the fish

Fish are usually placed in a clear plastic bag because this is a safer way of transporting them than using a small tank, as the water could easily spill in transit. The bag is usually partly filled with water from the tank where the fish are housed, then the fish are caught in a net and transferred to the bag. The bag is filled with oxygen, sealed, and placed within a second bag.

Stand the bag in darkened conditions, such as in a cardboard box or another plastic bag, for the journey home. A box is probably the best option, especially if you are travelling by car. Place it directly behind one of the front seats, with the bag carefully set so that it stays upright and will not tip over or move around. Keeping them in this part of the car also ensures that the fish are in a relatively shaded position.

Caution • Never leave fish alone in a car, particularly on a hot day. The temperature can rise rapidly in your absence, which could prove fatal for them. Keep the journey time to a minimum, so you can transfer them to their new environment without delay.

The importance of isolation

At first, it is best to settle the fish in a separate isolation tank for about two weeks, so you can ensure that they are eating well and showing no signs of illness. If there are any problems, they can be contained or resolved much more easily in isolation, saving you time, money, and effort in the long term. It does not need to be an elaborate set-up, but obviously it will need a heater and filter. This will in any case be useful in future as well, as emergency accommodation if you need to transfer fish out of the main aquarium, or as a spawning tank.

Gentle introduction

When you arrive home with the fish, start by floating them in their bag on the surface of the water for about 20 minutes. This makes the water temperature in the bag rise gently again so that it is in equilibrium with

You should use a special aquarium thermometer to test the water temperature in the tank. The digital models shown here display the temperature range in colour, and have adhesive backing that allows them to be fixed to the outside of the tank.

that in the tank. Always avoid subjecting fish to sudden shifts in temperature, which may be stressful and harmful, so never put them straight into water that might be several degrees warmer than that in the bag.

Float the fish's bag on the water so that the temperature within gradually rises to match that in the tank.

Avoiding new tank syndrome

A totally sterile aquarium is not a good environment for fish. Without the presence of beneficial aerobic bacteria, the breakdown of their waste through the nitrogen cycle cannot take place. Instead, decomposing waste builds up in their environment, and if unchecked, deaths resulting from so-called 'new tank syndrome' will inevitably result.

You therefore need to prepare the aquarium to receive them in advance, by adding a special bacterial culture, preferably about a week before you introduce the fish. This interval also gives the plants a chance to become established in the tank. Remember that you must leave the filtration system running constantly, although the fish are not yet in the tank, in order to encourage the development of the bacteria; lighting is similarly essential for the plants' survival.

Checking the filter system

If a canister filter fails to operate immediately, do not panic, because this may simply be due to an air lock in the system. Switch it off, remove it from the water, and dismantle the unit as you would to service it. Then put it back together again, and it should function properly.

Transfer the fish carefully with a net. Do not tip in water from the bag – it could introduce harmful microbes into the tank.

WARNING

When you open the bag, do not simply pour the water with the fish straight into the tank. Either place the bag in an empty bucket or ask someone else to hold the bag open, while you carefully net the fish and transfer them to the aquarium. Discard the water left in the bag, to minimize any risk of introducing harmful microbes from the previous tank into their new home.

Temperature check

At this initial stage, you should also ensure that the heaterstat maintains the water temperature correctly, making any adjustments as necessary. Use an aquarium thermometer to give you an accurate reading, siting it well away from the heater itself. There are two main types: alcohol-filled models which attach inside the tank, and digital models which fix to the outside of the glass. Digital designs are more widely used because they are generally reliable, easier to read, and cannot be attacked by fish, although if touched – by children, for example – they may give a falsely high reading.

Keep the aquarium lights switched off for several hours, to help nervous fish to settle down in their new surroundings.

Catching fish

Not surprisingly, fish will try to avoid being caught, so unless you proceed in the right way, you may cause great disruption in the tank when trying to catch them. Take particular care when catching fish in a community aquarium, because your attempts to net one type of fish may alarm the others and result in their attempting to take evasive action. They could even leap out of the tank undetected, while you are concentrating on catching their companions (see box, far right). When catching fish, remember to wear gloves as always when dipping your hands into the aquarium.

Using a net

Catching nets are produced in a range of sizes, so make sure you obtain one of suitable dimensions. A large net may sound like a good idea, theoretically making it easier to catch the fish, but in fact it is nowhere near as manoeuvrable as a smaller net in the confines of a tank. You need agility to match that of the fish, and a large net is almost bound to impede you by snagging on rockwork and other decor, or even disturbing the plants.

To catch fish, you will need a suitably sized net. Try to give yourself as much space as possible in the tank, even removing some of the rockwork and other decor if necessary.

Select a net that will allow you to scoop fish into it individually – in most cases, a 10cm (4in) net should be adequate, although obviously, the best size to use also depends on the size of the fish. You should never attempt to catch a large fish with a small net because this could cause injury.

Catching smaller fish

If you need to catch smaller, fast-swimming fish, the best approach is to ambush them from below, rather than chasing them round and round the aquarium with the net, which will be disruptive at the very least. First, place the net in the tank, lowering it right into the depths in the relatively open area of water at the front. Then either drop a little food on the surface to attract the fish, or try to steer them towards the area above the net using a clean piece of wooden dowelling. At this point, you should be able to scoop them up easily from beneath; if you try to catch them from behind, there is much more drag on the net in the water, and they will be able to elude capture fairly readily.

Always aim to place the net beneath the fish, scooping it up from below. If you try to chase after it from the side, this will be more difficult and more disruptive within the tank.

Special techniques

A net is not always the best tool for catching fish, and in some cases it could even be counterproductive, especially with fish that have a snake-like shape, such as the spiny eel (*Macrognathus aculeatus*). If you try to catch this fish with a net, you may well find that it burrows into the substrate and simply disappears.

With this type of fish, a different method is recommended, which requires stealth and a certain degree of patience. Cut a piece of clean rubber hosing long enough and wide enough to accommodate the fish, and place this in an accessible position within the aquarium. Before long, the eel is bound to investigate this new hiding-place. Once the fish is inside, simply lift the tubing out of the tank, placing a finger over each end to prevent the fish from slipping out, before transferring it to its new surroundings.

The awkward shape of tall or deep-bodied fish such as angelfish (*Pterophyllum* species) makes them hard to net in the conventional way. If you do use a net, approach the fish with the net held vertically, to increase your chance of catching it. Another technique is to place a plastic bag in the water, holding the mouth open with one hand. Use the net to steer the fish into the bag, which you can then lift out of the water. These fish need plenty of oxygen, so if you will be moving them any distance, carefully bail some of the water out of the bag back into the aquarium, replacing it with air, before tying the top securely.

Spiny fish

Take particular care with spiny fish, such as the coolie loach. Spines often serve to help protect fish from predators, which spit them out once they have trouble swallowing them, and they also impede attempts to catch the fish. Coolie loaches have spines near their eyes, which they dig into the net, often resulting in their becoming stuck. If you try to force them out of the net, you might injure them, so simply invert the net in the water, and the fish should free itself quickly and swim away.

Make sure the power supply is switched off before you put your hands in the water. Wearing gloves to protect yourself from any risk of infection in the water, place one hand over the top of the net to prevent the fish from jumping out.

Initial concerns

Once you have established a maintenance routine, caring for your fish can be fairly straightforward. In the first few weeks after you have introduced the fish, however, the new aquarium will require more attention, primarily to prevent the risk of deaths from new tank syndrome. As previously mentioned, this problem arises when the fish produce more waste than the new bacteria in the filter system can break down.

Testing for ammonia

If there is a build-up of ammonia in the water, from waste that has not been effectively broken down, this is toxic to the fish. Effects may include damage to the lining of the intestinal tract, interference with the correct functioning of the nervous system, and harm to the gills. You can buy a test kit to check the ammonia level, but the results need to be considered in relation to the water's pH. In an alkaline aquarium, the effect of ammonia is significantly greater due to a chemical reaction, so tropical fish in these conditions are therefore most vulnerable to new tank syndrome. Temperature also has an effect, with toxic levels of free ammonia rising more rapidly at higher temperatures.

Nitrite

Some of the tank's beneficial bacteria are *Nitrosomonas* bacteria, which use oxygen to convert harmful free ammonia to nitrite (NO_2). While nitrite is in general far less toxic than ammonia, some fish are still very susceptible to it in high levels. For example, discus (*Symphysodon discus*) are vulnerable at a nitrite reading of just 0.5mg/litre, although many tropical fish are unaffected until the concentration is 10–20mg/litre. Effects of nitrite are most pronounced in soft water.

Nitrite poisoning affects the fish in a highly specific way: it acts on the red blood cells, modifying the haemoglobin which carries oxygen around the body, preventing this reaction from taking place. Fish suffering from nitrite toxicity have gills that are brown rather than reddish as a result.

Nitrate

The production of nitrate occurs due to the action of different bacteria – the *Nitrobacter* species. Nitrate is not generally a problem as far as freshwater tropical fish are concerned, although fry are more susceptible to a build-up than adult fish. Two exceptions are discus and fish living in brackish water, neither of which will thrive in

high nitrate conditions. The simplest way to combat the problem is to carry out regular partial water changes. This is especially important at first, until the filter systems are fully functional.

It is not just the fish's waste that can influence the levels of nitrate. Uneaten food has the same effect, which is partly why fish should not be fed more than they will consume within a few minutes.

PARTIAL WATER CHANGES

It is vital for the health of the fish that you change a proportion of the water in the tank on a regular basis, partly because it helps to prevent a build-up of nitrate in the water. It is usually recommended to change up to one-quarter of the water every two weeks, particularly in the first months after setting up the tank. Replace it with water that has been treated with a conditioner and is at the same temperature as that within the aquarium. The easiest way to carry out a partial water change is to use an aquarium siphon, which simply transfers water to a bucket placed on the floor.

A purpose-designed aquarium siphon makes it easy to carry out a partial water change. Remember to treat the tap water you initially add to the siphon with a dechlorinator.

Safe siphoning

When siphoning out the water, never, ever start the flow through the tube by sucking the lower end, or you could end up seriously ill. Instead, fill the tubing with conditioned water, using a watering can with a narrow spout, and place a thumb over each end. Then put one end in the aquarium, removing your thumb here only once the end is below the water level, and taking care to prevent the tube from lifting out of the water.

Once the other end of the tube is safely in the bucket, release the pressure of your other thumb, and the water should then flow into the bucket. When the right amount of water has been siphoned off and you want to stop the flow, place your thumb back over the lower end, lift the tube up into the aquarium so that the water can drain out, and then remove it.

Battery siphons and gravel cleaners

You can also buy battery-operated siphons, but the flow is sometimes less predictable, particularly if gravel becomes accidentally sucked into the machine, which may prove hard to dislodge. A useful additional piece of equipment which may be operated in conjunction

WARNING

Remember, you must **always** switch off and disconnect the power supply before placing your hand in the water; without this precaution, you could receive a fatal shock if there were some kind of fault. Wear suitable disposable gloves when carrying out a partial water change to:
• protect you from the slight risk of contracting a skin granuloma from a piscine tuberculosis infection.
• ensure that no other potentially harmful microbes can enter your body via any cuts or abrasions.
• protect the fish from the risk of accidental poisoning from any contaminants that might be on your hands.

with the siphon is a gravel cleaner. This helps to prevent the filter bed from becoming stagnant, with a resulting decline in numbers of beneficial bacteria. It stirs up the gravel and removes the mulm (decaying organic matter), without sucking up the substrate medium. A plastic cup at the base keeps disturbance within the aquarium to a minimum, so that plants will not be uprooted.

Some of these siphons are multi-purpose, acting also as a gravel cleaner and reducing the strain on the filter system. The gravel is stirred up, releasing mulm which is sucked up.

This type of siphon causes virtually no disturbance within the aquarium, and should not harm the fish. After siphoning, lift the tube out of the tank, letting the water drain into the bucket.

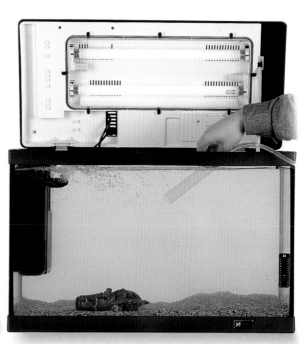

Routine maintenance

Establishing a care routine will help you keep the ecosystem within your aquarium in balance, and the inhabitants in good health. As well as partial water changes (see pages 80–81), maintenance usually includes periodically removing algae, cleaning, caring for plants, and looking after your equipment, such as cleaning or changing the filter wool, so that it functions properly.

Controlling algae

A certain amount of algae is healthy, but it does need to be kept in check. Some fish, and aquatic snails, browse on algae, but if it still starts to spread onto the sides of the tank, you may need to shorten the time that the aquarium lights are on each day. Watch for signs of algae growing on the leaves of other plants in the tank, because it threatens their growth by blocking the pores here. Some plants are more susceptible than others, with the fine net-like leaves of the Madagascar lace plant (*Aponogeton madagascariensis*) especially vulnerable to colonization by algae. This ultimately

At times, you may need to clean excess algae from the sides of the tank using an aquarium scraper or stiff brush.

dual-pad scraper

glass scraper

acrylic scraper

makes the leaves rot, killing the plant.

There are magnetic or long-handled scrapers which you can use to clean off excess algae. Take extra care with an acrylic tank or you may scratch it. Aside from being unsightly, these scratches may then also be invaded by algae, creating green streaks that are almost impossible to remove without emptying the tank and scrubbing the affected areas. If you spot algae in the airlift or a similar site, then use a small bottle brush to clear the tubing.

While green algae predominate where there is too much light, you may find brownish growth in a tank that is underlit, especially if has no living plants. This is usually most seen on rockwork; remove the rock and clean off the algae with a scrubbing brush and water.

Cleaning

Overall cleanliness within the aquarium will be helped by sloping the substrate slightly; with the movement of the fish, mulm that is not drawn up into the filter will collect at the front of the tank, and can be siphoned out.

Using a gravel cleaner is particularly important with catfish; if the substrate becomes dirty, their barbels may become infected or develop body ulcers where they rest in contact with the bottom. Certain bottom-dwelling species of catfish may also aggravate the problem of excess algae and harm plants. These fish tend to stir up any mulm in the substrate, which resettles on the plants' leaves, again blocking the pores, and encouraging algal growth on the plants.

Plant care and management

It is very common for plants, however lush they may appear at first, to fail to some extent soon after being moved to a new aquarium. Do not be tempted to discard them because, assuming that the conditions are generally favourable for them in terms of water and light, they should start to rejuvenate and grow well. As well as light and nitrate, the plants also need a range of minerals and trace elements for their well-being. For example, iron deficiency tends to turn the leaves white before the plant stops growing. This is especially common with *Echinodorus* species, as well as certain types of *Vallisneria*. Plants need iron to make chlorophyll, used in photosynthesis, so you may have to provide a specific fertilizer that contains it. Partial water changes (see pages 80–1) are important for plants as well as for the fish, helping to ensure that key trace elements found in tap water are regularly replaced.

EQUIPMENT CARE

Apart from raking over the filter bed occasionally, an undergravel filter needs virtually no attention. You should make a regular check that the air pump is working correctly – without oxygen, the bacterial population will die off, and, unless this is detected, the ammonia level will rise with deadly results

Should the air supply become impaired, check first that the tubing is not kinked or squashed. If you notice the air pump becoming noisier, have it serviced, although you will need a replacement to keep the system running while it is being checked. Make sure that the air pump is never covered, because this could start a fire.

Filters

If you have a box, sponge, or canister filter with a core containing a filter medium, you will have to maintain the filter wool in good condition, so that it does not impede the flow of water. How often you need to do this varies, depending on the strain imposed on the filter by the volume and condition of the water.

Bacteria • The existing filter wool will include an established colony of beneficial bacteria, so in general it is better to wash it, rather than replace it, otherwise

One way of removing algae is to use a magnetic cleaner; a magnet outside the glass pulls scrapers over the inside. It is useful for large areas, but you will need a brush for corners.

A typical power filter, opened up to show the central core. This kind of filter sits in the water, and is available in a range of sizes, suitable for different tanks.

water exits via nozzle

filter sponge for bacteria

water is drawn in via casing slit

filtration will be poor until new bacteria establish.

Washing filter wool • Do not use fresh tap water since it contains chlorine, which acts as a disinfectant, killing the bacteria. Instead, use some of the old water siphoned out of the tank, squeezing the wool or sponge to remove the dirt. Replace the wool and reassemble the filter.

Changing filter wool • After a time, the filter wool will start to deteriorate and should be changed; it is best to replace it gradually, removing some of the old wool and adding a new portion alongside. This minimizes the effects on the bacterial population, although you may also add a bacterial culture at this stage, to speed up the maturation of the new filter.

Peat filter • Peat used in a filter needs to be changed regularly. In a new tank especially, it is wise to switch

double-sided magnetic cleaner, seen from above

Breeding

As you become more experienced in fish-keeping, and more knowledgeable about the needs of your fish, you may want to try your hand at breeding them. Successful breeding in the home aquarium can be immensely rewarding, although it is unlikely to be financially worthwhile! With some species, it is relatively straightforward to encourage them to breed, while others represent a serious challenge; for this reason, many breeders decide to specialize in a particular species so they can develop their expertise.

If you plan to breed fish even on a small scale, you will need to invest in further tanks and equipment, and therefore require extra space. Keen enthusiasts may even establish a devoted 'fish house', a specially built unit planned to accommodate their aquaria where young fish may be reared in spacious surroundings.

Colour changes

One of the clearest and most reliable indicators of the onset of breeding condition is a change in the fish's appearance. Check whether this applies to any of the species you want to breed, so you can be alert for it.

AGGRESSION

Both sexes tend to be more active than usual before or during spawning, and they may show signs of aggression towards other fish, especially others of their own kind, or species with similar coloration. Individual fish do differ in temperament, however, with some proving to be noticeably more aggressive than others of the same species at spawning time. The risk of aggression is generally greatest where males outnumber females in a shoal, although this may be hard to avoid because it is usually impossible to sex the fish at the time of purchase. Once the spawning period is past, harmony in the aquarium should be restored.

A number of fish become more colourful as they become ready to spawn, particularly the males. Cherry barbs (*Barbus titteya*), for example, become a much richer shade of red at this stage. Females also swell in size due to their eggs, a change you should notice most clearly when you see the fish from the side.

TRIGGERING SPAWNING

Fish may breed at any time of the year, although you can often encourage them to spawn by making changes in their environment or diet. Success depends in part on replicating the natural triggers, such as a falling water level in the case of annual killifish, or a slight drop in the water temperature, mimicking the effect of an influx of fresh rain water during the wet season which causes rivers and streams to swell. Feeding can also have an impact, with an increased amount of live food (see page 94–5) often being used to encourage breeding. Some fish may also exhibit changes in their normal behaviour.

Various factors may trigger reproduction in fish, such as changes in water level, as happens with these pacus (Colossoma macropromus) in the Amazon.

Water changes

Spawning triggers differ to some extent from species to species, and not all are equally easy to replicate. A technique worth trying with fish from the Amazon, such as tetras, involves mirroring the natural changes in their water conditions. The water level in the Amazon River and its tributaries may vary considerably through the year. During the dry season, the fish congregate in the remaining areas of water, which contain a greater concentration of pollutants such as decaying vegetation and fish waste.

Once the rains come, the influx of fresh water raises the water level, dilutes the existing water, and lowers the temperature slightly. The increased volume of water, less polluted environment, and resulting proliferation of insect life in the water, triggers reproductive behaviour, with the fish starting to spawn in these conditions within a few weeks.

In an aquarium, you can simply mimic these changes by carrying out a partial water change, raising the water level and reducing the temperature slightly. Adding blackwater extract, which helps to soften the water, is also often recommended for tetras and similar fish in the build-up to spawning activity.

A note of caution

If your aquarium contains any fish that you have acquired recently, then it is not a good idea to lower the water temperature, because this could be stressful for them. The immune system of fish responds better at higher temperatures, and if they become chilled, they are more vulnerable to opportunistic infections such as fungus. If you have a community aquarium, it may therefore simply be better to transfer the ones you want to breed to a spawning tank, and adjust the heaterstat here for a slightly lower temperature.

Feeding changes

Changing the fish's food often serves as another potential breeding trigger. It will typically take a fortnight or so for the fish to respond to this change in diet before they show signs of spawning activity.

Sexing is easy with some species, such as with these giant cichlids (Petenia splendida). *The male, above, is considerably larger and has more intense markings than the female, below.*

- In the wild, the increase in insect life stimulates many species to come into breeding condition. To mimic this, offer the fish more fresh, invertebrate-based foods, rather than formulated foods.
- Beware of using insects or other creatures gathered from the wild, because these can introduce disease to the aquarium (see page 94). It is better to culture your own supplies of live foods.
- There are also special conditioning foods, which are used in conjunction with the fish's normal diet.

Spawning activity

Even if you have provided a stimulus, you may still be caught unawares by the fish; if they appear more active than usual in the morning, with the male pursuing the female intently, then spawning may well be imminent. If you want to try to control spawning time, you could position the spawning tank so it catches the early morning sun. Take care, especially during the summer, not to site it where it is in full sun for any length of time, however, or the fish will become overheated.

Preparing for breeding

When it comes to breeding fish, paying attention to detail will greatly improve your chances of success. Bear in mind that relatively few fish display any signs of parental care, so it is up to you to protect the eggs or fry from being eaten by the adults. It is worth setting up a separate spawning tank so you can create the ideal conditions to suit a particular species. Spawning is a stressful activity, especially for the female, so provide the pair with a nutritious diet to restore their condition. This will also improve the chances of their spawning successfully in future.

Filtration and lighting

Take care not to overfeed the female while she is confined, because any uneaten food will pollute the tank, endangering the health of the fry in due course. Young fish tend to be more vulnerable to ammonia and other nitrogenous products in the water than adults.

Filtration within breeding tanks is therefore of particular importance. A foam filter is usually the best choice; unlike a power filter, its gentle movements are unlikely to pose any hazard to the young fish.

Undergravel filters • This type of filter is not feasible in the short term, because of the length of time that it takes for the filter bed to mature.

Improving filtration • If desired, use a special bacterial culture to help to speed up the biological activity of a foam filter.

Tank decor • On grounds of hygiene, keep decor in the breeding tank to a minimum, otherwise there is an increased risk of outbreaks of fungus, for example, which are especially likely to be harmful in the period that any eggs are developing in the tank.

Lighting • This is not needed over the spawning tank, especially in the case of tetras – their eggs are adversely affected by exposure to bright light.

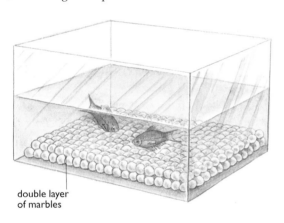

double layer of marbles

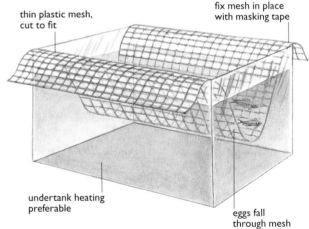

thin plastic mesh, cut to fit

fix mesh in place with masking tape

undertank heating preferable

eggs fall through mesh

Unfortunately, the parental instincts of many fish are not highly developed, so you will need to take steps to protect the eggs from being eaten by their parents. Options include laying marbles on the floor or fixing plastic mesh so the eggs fall through to safety beneath. Some species prefer to lay their eggs in plants or under flowerpots or rockwork.

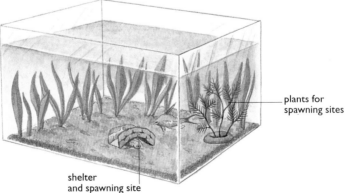

plants for spawning sites

shelter and spawning site

Breeding livebearers

In the case of livebearers, such as guppies, a number of the fry will be eaten by the other fish, including their own mother, although some offspring may survive in a densely planted tank. A simple way of avoiding this problem is to transfer the female to a breeding trap in a separate tank. This allows the fry to escape through the trap, while the mother is too large to follow. The breeding tank may be relatively small, with a gravel base and plants incorporated into one half.

   Aim to move the female into a separate tank before she shows signs of giving birth, otherwise there is a real risk that she will abort her brood prematurely. As the time for producing her brood approaches, she will start to swell in size, with a definite black spot appearing on her flanks.

Some pairs of discus (Symphysodon discus) *may eat their own eggs rather than guard them. In such cases, you should protect the eggs with a mesh barrier, as shown here.*

EGG-LAYERS

The tank set-up should be influenced by the breeding behaviour of the particular type of fish. Tank dividers can be useful with egg-layers, especially for species where the male tends to harass the female. This helps you ensure that both fish are equally ready to breed before you put them together. Some species lay their eggs on rockwork, so provide this where necessary.

Safeguarding the eggs

Fish that are likely to consume their eggs should be housed in such a way that the eggs are placed out of their reach as soon as possible after laying.

Plastic mesh • One way to achieve this aim is with a guard of thin plastic mesh, sunk in a U-shape into the tank. The eggs will fall through the mesh, out of reach. When putting this mesh in place, allow enough space for the fish to swim and spawn easily. Check that it fits snugly at each end, so none of the adults can slip through. After egg-laying, transfer the adults back to the main aquarium, and remove the mesh.

Marbles • With larger egg-layers, it is better to line the floor of the tank with marbles – the tiny gaps allow the eggs to slip down to relative safety. Only half-fill the tank, setting the heaterstat accordingly, before placing the fish in their spawning quarters.

Plants for spawning

Certain egg-layers, such as tetras, actively seek to spawn in plants, rather than scattering their eggs at random around their quarters. In the spawning tank, you should include either artificial spawning mops, or plants with feathery leaves, like fanworts (*Cabomba* species). Mops have the advantage of being more sterile than plants. Arrange the spawning mops or plants to provide fairly dense cover, since the fish will swim in and spawn among the strands or foliage, leaving their adhesive eggs sticking to them.

Bubble-nest builders

If setting up a breeding tank for gouramis and related species, you should cover it to prevent the newly-hatched fry from becoming chilled. Include floating plants, as an anchorage point for the bubble-nest which will be constructed by the male. Once this stage is reached, you can introduce the female, and spawning should take place shortly afterwards.

   Once the female has laid the eggs, she should be removed, leaving the male to guard the eggs. At first, you should not use any filtration in the tank, because it can easily destroy the delicate bubble-nest, but you will need to introduce it at a later stage.

Rearing the fry

To safeguard your next generation of fish, you need to be especially attentive during the hatching of the eggs and for the critical first few days after the fry emerge. The hatching period depends not only on the species, but also on the water temperature. In most cases, the fry hatch within a couple of days, although there are exceptions, such as with annual killifish (see pages 36–7).

At first, you may not even notice the first fry to hatch, because they are not free-swimming immediately. Instead, they rest on the floor of the breeding tank or among the plants, using up the remains of their yolk sacs from the eggs. This sac, which you can see on the underside of the body, provides the fry with nutrients.

FEEDING FRY

Once the young fish start to become free-swimming, they need to find food for themselves. You can supply them with various types of proprietary foods to help meet their nutritional requirements at this stage. Choose a food specifically intended for the type of fish you are rearing, to ensure that the particles are of an appropriate size to suit the fry. Livebearers' offspring are generally quite large compared with the fry of egg-layers, so can generally eat larger pieces of food. Anabantoids are among the smallest fry and they must be given food small enough for them to cope with or

Young discus feed on a special secretion produced on the sides of their parents' bodies. This helps to make their chances of survival through the first crucial days of life less precarious.

Egg-laying fish produce hundreds, even thousands, of eggs, because only a very few will survive to maturity. The fry do not swim free at once; first, they absorb their yolk sacs.

they will starve in the critical early days after they become free-swimming. In some cases, however, the actual body size of the fry does not correlate closely to the size of the mouth.

Growing food

If obtaining commercial fry foods is difficult, or as a supplementary source of food, you can grow your own cultures very easily. You should set these up in advance of the anticipated spawning in order to be prepared. The first food fry consume are known as infusoria – tiny microbes that develop in a jar of water. Include some vegetable matter in the jar, preferably organically grown, to avoid the risk of chemical contamination. The protozoa and other microbes forming the infusoria do

---

WARNING

Some fish-breeders like to introduce aquatic live foods such as *Daphnia* (see page 94) to the diet of their young fish, but this may be a risky strategy, even if these insects are sieved out of the water first. Harmful microbes in the water may be introduced to the tank – in an extreme case, these could wipe out an entire brood, just at the stage when their care should be becoming easier.

not survive well in heated water, so must be cultured outside the tank then added subsequently.

Making an infusoria culture
• Leave a jar of ordinary tap water without a lid for a day, then add a lettuce leaf or a small amount of straw.
• Place it in bright light, on a window sill for example. The water will turn cloudy within a few days, indicating that the microbes are developing.
• To feed the fry, suck up some of the water and place it close to the fish in their aquarium. Young fish cannot swim far, so direct their food within easy reach at first.
• Feed them small amounts on a regular basis. Set this up on a drip flow if you have to be out for long periods.

Brine shrimp

For feeding larger fry, small crustaceans called brine shrimp (*Artemia salina*) are often used. These are available as eggs, which you combine with salt water according to the accompanying instructions, in order to make them hatch for a fresh supply of fry food.

The hatching rate may vary, and it will improve your yield if you aerate the water initially; this should help the eggs' thick outer casing to become saturated, which is essential if they are to hatch. At a temperature of about 25°C (77°F), hatching should occur within a day or two. Set up several cultures, each spaced two or three days apart, to ensure you will have a constant supply.

The young that hatch, called nauplii, are the larval form in the life cycle of the brine shrimp. You need to establish enough cultures to provide food for roughly seven to 10 days, after which the fish can be transferred onto powdered flake or similar foods.

You can carefully siphon out the brine shrimp which have hatched as they will be in the main body of the water, whereas the indigestible shells and unhatched eggs will remain on the bottom. Sieve the nauplii and

You can buy a hatching kit for brine shrimp or use a suitable receptacle, which should be rinsed with tap water, then treated with a dechlorinator.

shrimp eggs

tube bung to keep eggs dry

dunk them in dechlorinated fresh water, to remove the inevitable salty residue, before offering them to the fish.

Other rearing foods

Another food that is valuable for rearing purposes are microworms. These are cultured in a similar way to whiteworm (see pages 94–5), with cultures being set up sequentially. It takes 10–14 days for a culture to provide a harvestable quantity of microworms.

In an emergency, you can use finely sieved egg yolk as an alternative. Push the yolk through muslin to produce miniscule particles suitable for the fry. Only use this food with caution, however, because too much will pollute the water.

HOUSING THE FRY

Before long, presuming that you have successfully reared a large number of fry, you will need to split them up and transfer them into other tanks. If they become overcrowded, this will stunt their growth and lead to a rapid build-up of pollutants in the tank which will make them more vulnerable to illness.

It is advisable to separate the fish into batches partly based on their size, otherwise fast-growing individuals of cannibalistic species such as piranhas (*Serrasalmus* species) will start to feed on their smaller fellows. Some losses will be inevitable, however, even with the best care. You should also weed out any obviously deformed individuals – with badly formed tails, for example – and destroy these humanely. In the wild, these would inevitably fall victim to predators.

With species that do provide parental care for their offspring, it obviously adds greatly to the interest of breeding them if you can observe this behaviour at close quarters. As well as the breeding tank, remember that you will also need to set up alternative accommodation for when the time comes for you to separate the adult fish from their brood.

Brine shrimp are sold in the form of eggs, which are collected from the large salt lakes; these eggs are hatched at home to provide fresh food for fry.

Feeding

With the wide range of formulated foods available nowadays, including general-purpose diets as well as specialist kinds for different fish groups, feeding aquarium fish has become relatively easy. Many live foods may also be obtained fresh, freeze-dried, or frozen, but if you prefer, you can grow your own for a ready fresh supply .

Digestion and feeding habits

Fish have a range of feeding habits, so find out how the species you intend to keep would normally eat in the wild; this enables you to meet their needs as closely as possible. The two main groups are herbivores and carnivores, but within these divisions there are numerous other preferences and habits.

Take care not to overfeed your fish, because uneaten food may contaminate the water. Feed them little and often – two to three small amounts each day, with the final feed last thing at night if you have any nocturnal species. In a community aquarium, also take account of which levels the fish inhabit – providing floating foods for surface-feeders and sinking ones for bottom-dwellers.

THE DIGESTIVE SYSTEM

There is a key difference between most species of tropical aquarium fish and cyprinids, such as barbs and danios. Unlike other fish, cyprinids have no stomach; instead, the first part of the intestinal tract can be distended with food, until it is digested through the tract.

Cyprinids use their pharyngeal teeth, located at the back of the throat, to grind food morsels into smaller particles, so they can swallow it. The food travels down the oesophagus into the intestine, where an enzyme called trypsin helps digest protein, Other fish also use pepsin, produced in the stomach, for this purpose.

Enzymes and bile enter the digestive tract at the end of the oesophagus. This does not occur in fish with true stomachs because the stomach acid would inactivate these enzymes. In cyprinids, this mixing of enzymes and food for a long period improves their digestive efficiency, so that they can derive the maximum benefit from the available nutrients.

Breakdown of foodstuffs

In cyprinids, these chemicals start to act on food stored in the intestinal sac. Some enzymes assist the uptake of protein, while others help to break down carbohydrate, converting it into the fish's main source of energy. Bile assists in the breakdown and absorption of fats.

Protein in the diet is important for growth, and it can help trigger spawning behaviour in adult fish (see pages 84–5). Fats provide a good source of energy, and are a key component of cell membranes, as well as aiding the manufacture of hormones.

The length of time taken for food to pass through the fish's digestive tract is influenced by the temperature of the surroundings, and the length of the tract itself.

Carnivores • Carnivorous fish have a short intestinal tract, because they can absorb nutrients very efficiently; this is partly due to the production of

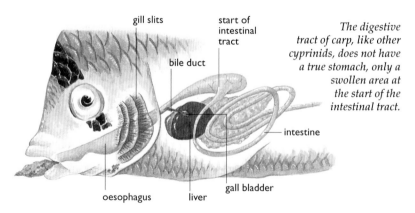

gill slits

start of intestinal tract

bile duct

intestine

The digestive tract of carp, like other cyprinids, does not have a true stomach, only a swollen area at the start of the intestinal tract.

oesophagus

liver

gall bladder

The suckermouth catfish uses its mouth not just for anchorage but also to rasp at algae and rotting wood as part of its diet.

collagenase, an additional enzyme which assists with the breakdown of animal protein.

Herbivores • Herbivorous fish have long digestive tracts so they can digest and absorb the nutrients from their vegetarian diet, because there is considerably less protein in this type of food.

FEEDING HABITS AND PREFERENCES

In a community aquarium, you will probably have to provide a range of foods to suit different fish, even within a group, fish may have different needs. Rift Valley cichlids, for example, have remarkably diverse feeding habits although they inhabit the same environment. This enables them to survive at much higher densities than they could otherwise, simply because they do not compete with each other for a single food source.

In Lake Malawi alone, there are more than 400 species of cichlid. Some are herbivorous, others predatory, and there is considerable diversity within these categories. Certain vegetarian species graze on algae found on rocks by the lake shore, while others feed on plankton in the water, or consume larger plants. Insects are a major part of the diet for other cichlids in the lake, while some are active hunters and will cannibalize their own kind.

Suitable foods

Consider not just which type of food the fish eat, but also how they obtain their food. If you provide small worms for hatchetfish, for example, you need to put the worms in a floating holder to keep them near the surface, or they will sink. Hatchetfish feed at the surface

and rarely venture down to the lower reaches for food, any more than Corydoras catfish will scout at the surface. Look out for special foods designed to meet the specific dietary preferences and feeding habits of different fish, such as foods that sink to the bottom of the aquarium which are suitable for catfish.

Watch for predators

A fish's shape gives an indication of its feeding habits: for example, predatory catfish are typically much more streamlined than their bottom-dwelling cousins, a sign that they swim fast to hunt prey. There are exceptions, however: some predators are relatively passive and use camouflage to lure unsuspecting prey within reach.

Obviously, do not mix fish that might prey on each other. When adding new fish, investigate not just their potential size, but also their feeding habits. Remember, some fish hunt only at night, so you may not realize their predatory nature until you notice that one or more of their companions has disappeared in the morning!

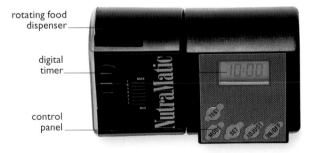

rotating food dispenser

digital timer

control panel

A battery-operated, automatic fish-feeder can be very useful for dispensing pre-set amounts of food into the tank if you are away for a prolonged period.

Formulated foods

There is now a tremendous choice of formulated foods available for tropical fish, including general-purpose diets, specialist products for specific fish groups, and colour foods, which enhance red coloration. Formulated foods have greatly simplified the keeping and breeding of tropical fish in home aquaria, increasing the hobby's popularity. A general flake food is suitable for most inhabitants in a typical community aquarium, but you might need to supplement it with an alternative diet for certain fish; bottom-dwelling catfish, for example, need to be given a food that sinks.

PROVIDING A BALANCED DIET

Just like us, many fish benefit from a broad and varied diet, but you may not find it practical to supply them with a range of fresh foods prepared in tiny morsels. Overall, their diet should include protein for growth and cell regeneration; carbohydrates and fats, primarily for energy; fibre to keep the digestive tract in good order; and the right vitamins and minerals to maintain their general health and resistance to disease.

The prime advantage of formulated foods is convenience, and, provided you choose a food suitable for the fish you keep, it should contain all the nutrients necessary to keep the fish in good health. If you have carnivorous fish, you may also want to supplement their diet with live foods (see pages 94–5).

Proteins and amino acids

It is not only carnivores that need protein – omnivorous and herbivorous fish must also have protein in their diet, although often in smaller amounts. The protein content of a fish's diet should range from roughly

35–50 percent, often more if you want to trigger spawning behaviour. Young individuals that are still growing need a higher proportion of protein.

Protein includes amino acids that are vital for growth. A good formulated food should contain the ten 'essential' amino acids that fish need in the correct amounts. Scientists are currently investigating the possibility of culturing microbes to incorporate into fish food with the required amino acid profile, rather than using fish meal for this purpose, as at present.

Carbohydrates and fats

A balance between key ingredients in fish food is important, because of the different functions fulfilled by proteins, carbohydrates, and fats. To make the situation more complex, different groups of fish do not require exactly the same balance of foods.

With a complete food, fish cannot choose what they eat, as they could in the wild. If the food contains too much carbohydrate, for example, this will be converted into fat in the body, causing the fish to become obese. Conversely, if the proportion of carbohydrate is too low, then the fish will be forced to use some of the protein in its diet to meet its energy requirement. As a result, its growth rate is then likely to suffer. An average fish diet should include up to about 15 percent carbohydrate and only about 10 percent of fats.

Vitamins and minerals

In addition to the major components of food, fish need vitamins and minerals to remain in good health. A well-balanced formulated food should include these in the right amounts. Different vitamins and minerals play

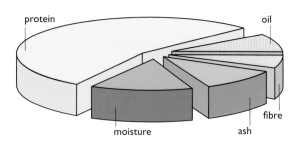

This pie chart shows the analysis of components of cichlid sticks.

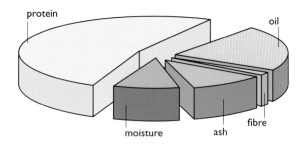

This chart illustrates an equivalent breakdown of catfish pellets.

particular roles – for example, B group vitamins are vital for the metabolism, A and E benefit the fish's immune system, while vitamin C also helps to improve resistance to infections.

In the past, manufacturers had problems incorporating vitamin C successfully into formulated foods, but they have now overcome these, so you can buy foods that include a stabilized form of vitamin C. An alternative is to use vitamin drops, which you add to the water in the tank. It is thought that the fish can benefit from this as they filter water through their bodies.

Various minerals also have a range of different functions in the body, ranging from calcium, which may be incorporated into bone, to iron, which is a key constituent of haemoglobin in the fish's red blood cells and so ensures that the blood can carry oxygen around the body. Like minerals, trace elements are similar inorganic chemicals, which are also important but are only required in much smaller quantities, as their name suggests.

The importance of fibre

The other significant constituent of a fish's food is fibre. Although fish are not dependent on fibre for nutritional value, it is vital to maintain the health of their digestive system. A deficiency of fibre may lead to an intestinal blockage. The obstruction is likely to constrict the swim-bladder, by pressing on it, and so will affect the balance of the fish in the water.

In the wild, fish may swallow some of the substrate, and not all the constituents of their diet will be digestible, such as the scales of fish consumed by carnivorous species. A well-balanced, formulated food may contain up to five percent of crude fibre by weight.

tablet food

floating flakes

cichlid sticks

catfish pellets

sinking wafers

Special diets

Where possible, use a special diet for your fish, although general-purpose flake food is used for most community aquarium fish. Some foods are designed for fish at certain stages: for example, growth foods for younger fish contain high levels of protein and vitamins.

Colour foods • Increasingly, these are based on natural crustacean ingredients, which intensify the fish's colour in the same way as in the wild, without artificial additives. Some colour foods may also help to stimulate successful spawning.

Conditioning foods • You may find these a valuable addition to the diet, especially in conjunction with other environmental changes, such as the use of blackwater extract, to encourage spawning.

Tablet foods • Usually suitable for both large and small fish, this type of food is given to fish that live at or near the bottom of the tank. Tablet foods have tended to replace pellets in recent years, being slower to break up on the substrate. Tablets may even stick to the aquarium glass, enabling you to watch the fish clearly as they feed here. Despite the name, do not confuse tablet foods with medicated foods.

Sinkers and floaters • Flake and food sticks float for a relatively long time, whereas granulated foods sink slowly within the tank, providing fish in the mid-water area with an opportunity to feed here.

Changing needs • As the fish grow, you will need to adjust their diet. At first, small vegetarian fish can be given flake food, but as they become bigger, offer floating food sticks, which they can swallow more easily.

There is a wide range of different types of prepared food available. Choose those that suit the feeding habits of your fish.

Live foods

Although formulated foods play a significant part in the diet of many fish, especially in a typical community aquarium set-up, live foods can also fulfil an important function. Live food is a key component in the diets of certain fish that do not thrive on formulated foods alone, and, in some cases, can act as a breeding trigger (the increased availability of protein-rich live food improves the chances of survival for fry, so the adult fish are stimulated to reproduce).

Many of these live foods, such as tubifex worms or daphnia, are available in prepared form, typically freeze-dried or frozen, while some may be obtained fresh. If using fresh worms, store them in a cool, dark place in a large container of water; they will not thrive within the confines of a glass jar. When offering worms to your fish, use a special feeder that sticks to the side of the tank, allowing the fish to eat the worms directly. If you simply tip them into the tank, then only the bottom-dwelling species are likely to benefit.

Aquatic live foods

Another live food traditionally offered to fish are water fleas. Usually known by their scientific name of *Daphnia*, these are actually tiny crustaceans and not fleas at all. Be warned that if you collect these from the wild such as from a pond, there is a risk of infection, and you could also inadvertently introduce hydra to your aquarium. This would be particularly devastating if you have any fry because the hydra will kill them rapidly with their stinging tentacles. One way to avoid this is to cultivate the daphnia yourself, in an old tank or similar container outdoors, so that they do not come into contact with other aquatic life.

Daphnia are available from aquatic stores in plastic bags of water. If they have been kept in direct sunlight, this can kill them very rapidly, so you should check that the majority of them are alive. Tap the sides of the bag and you should see them swimming around with their characteristic jerky movements.

Tip the bag into a small tank or similar container as soon as you reach home. You can then sieve the daphnia out of the water as you need them and transfer them to the aquarium. This is much safer than simply tipping the contents of the bag directly in alongside the fish. Daphnia are also sometimes used for their laxative effect; you can add them to the water as a remedy if any of your fish show signs of constipation, with their droppings trailing in a strand from their vent.

daphnia

Live foods such as daphnia may be bought at aquatic stores. Keep them cool; to use, sieve them out of the bag rather than tipping them directly into the tank.

Other aquatic live foods may be cultivated quite easily at home, using a bucket of water. This will attract gnats, for example, to lay their eggs here during summer. The eggs hatch into larvae which should be sieved out of the bucket then fed to the fish. As no other aquatic creatures are involved with this method, it is very unlikely that you will introduce any hazards to the tank.

TERRESTRIAL LIVE FOODS

A number of other live foods which have to be cultured rather than bought can be a valuable addition to the fish's diet. Starter cultures of whiteworm (*Enchytraeus*) and similar species are frequently available through advertisements in fish-keeping journals.

WARNING

There are a number of risks attached to feeding aquarium fish with live foods, particularly those of wild aquatic origin. Tubifex worms, for example are a very valuable form of live food for tropical aquarium fish, but bear in mind that these worms typically congregate in areas where there is plenty of organic matter in the water – such as around sewage outlets. While they can be carefully rinsed under running water, there is still a real risk that they could introduce disease-carrying micro-organisms or infection that could harm the fish.

Whiteworm

To culture your own whiteworms, first prepare a clean container with a lid, such as a margarine tub. Put in a small quantity of soil, then make drills in the soil with a pencil. Soak some bread in milk and poke this down into the drills. Divide up the starter culture, placing the worms on top of the food source, and cover them.

Transfer the culture to a reasonably warm place, ensuring that it does not dry out. Replace the bread every two or three days. After about a month, there should be enough worms to harvest. Separate them from the soil by tipping them into a saucer of water. You can then easily skim off the worms with tweezers and offer them to the fish in small quantities.

Fruit-flies

Fruit-fly (*Drosophila*) starter cultures are also available, which can be set up in large jam jars covered with muslin. Fruit-flies are especially appreciated by hatchetfish and other species that live close to the water surface. Try to obtain wingless fruit flies, because they will not escape into the home. Special feeding media are available, although you may also achieve good results by providing the flies with banana skins as a source of nutrients. To feed the fish, simply tip some of the flies directly onto the surface of the water. As with all live foods, do not add too much at once because leftover food will quickly pollute the water.

Earthworms

Another form of live food for fish that are available commercially are earthworms. Select the size carefully when placing your order, otherwise you will have to chop up the worms before offering them to your fish. In general, they are only suitable for larger species. It is best not to use worms directly from the garden, because there is a risk that they could have harmful microbes in their digestive tracts. If you do want to try using them, you should reduce this risk by leaving them in a moist container of vegetable matter for several days, in the hope that they will empty their digestive tracts.

Crickets

Various types of crickets are available in a range of sizes from small hatchlings upwards and so make a versatile live food. These are sold primarily for birds and reptiles, but may also be offered to fish. Feeding mealworms is less recommended, because their hard casing makes them relatively indigestible, although soft-bodied, white mealworms may be used safely.

Frozen packs of live foods are available in blister packs so you can use as much as you need and store the rest in a freezer.

bloodworms

tubifex worms

Prepared live foods

Many live foods are available in freeze-dried or frozen forms. Although relatively expensive, these foods may prove especially valuable for conditioning fish prior to breeding. They are also very convenient because they may be stored indefinitely without refrigeration and they are much safer to use than the equivalent fresh live food. Freeze-drying removes moisture from a food so that it keeps very well, without affecting its palatability too much. Small worms, such as bloodworm, are dried and compressed into blocks, whereas large river shrimp are frozen individually.

Gamma irradiated foodstuffs are sterilized and then frozen; they should be stored in a freezer. To use this food, cut off small blocks with a sharp knife as needed, and thaw them before feeding to the fish. If you only need part of a portion, you may be able to shave off pieces while still frozen so you thaw only a small amount.

Health care

Choosing healthy fish, providing them with good environmental conditions, and protecting them from undue stress are the keys to preventing unnecessary illness in your aquarium. It is also vital to spot and respond to any signs of disease or infection quickly, or the ailment may spread quickly to other fish in the tank.

How illness spreads

If you choose your stock well, and establish a good maintenance routine, you should find your fish remain generally healthy. Even the most experienced and attentive aquarist is bound to face some problems, however. Illness most often occurs with new arrivals, because the stress of the move tends to make them more vulnerable. Many fish carry bacteria and other microbes which normally cause them no ill-effects, but which may give problems when the fish are subjected to stress.

As well as watching your fish for pleasure, observe them at close quarters. Check that they are feeding properly, and appear healthy, with no unusual swellings or damage on their bodies. If you detect health problems at an early stage, it may well be possible to save the fish by simple treatment.

Prevention

To minimize potential problems, it is usually best to keep new acquisitions in a quarantine or isolation tank for at least two weeks, so you can check that they are feeding well and appear healthy. After this, you may transfer them to their permanent home. This initial settling-in stage can also be a potentially difficult period for the fish if they are introduced to an aquarium where other fish are already established. The newcomers may be regarded as intruders into this territory and may be harassed as a result. This may happen even in the case of fish that naturally form shoals, so watch them to make sure they are settling in well (see pages 76–7).

Initial precautions

It is always better to take precautions in the first place than to try to remedy problems once they occur:
• Check fish before you buy them (see pages 72–5), to reduce the risk of introducing illness to the aquarium.
• Discard the water in which you transported the fish, because it could contain potentially harmful microbes .
• Float the bag on the water in the new tank to equalize the temperatures. Fish are stressed by sudden changes in their conditions; if chilled, their immune system is less resistant to infections and fungus, especially if they are weak or if the scales or fins are damaged.
• Aquarium plants and substrate material may include hidden hazards, particularly parasites, so inspect plants carefully before adding them, and use an aquarium disinfectant to reduce the risk of infection.
• Once the fish are settled in, the greatest threat to their health, aside from poor water quality, comes from live foods of wild aquatic origin, which can introduce diseases and parasites to the tank.

Microscopic water-borne creatures such as this predatory green hydra may enter the tank along with aquatic live foods.

Stress can be a major factor in outbreaks of disease. Look out for signs of aggression, so that you can act to prevent harassment and avoid allowing your aquarium to become overcrowded.

The stress factor

Stress can be a major killer, especially when fish come into breeding condition. Watch for persistent bullying of weaker individuals at this time – if they do not get the chance to feed properly, they will become progressively weaker. Make sure the tank decor and planting allow fish the opportunity to find refuge when necessary. If you notice a particular fish being persecuted by a tankmate, one of the fish should be removed; it may be better to take out the dominant individual, reintroducing it at a later stage.

Care with chemicals

At times, you may encounter problems such as excess algae that you may want to tackle with chemicals. With any kind of chemical product, always follow the instructions strictly and only use a treatment recommended for aquarium use. Bear in mind that some products may have adverse side-effects on plants

or fish, so check that the product will not cause them any harm. Certain plants, especially any that have been colonized by algae, may be harmed by the use of an algicide.

Where possible, tackle problems using non-chemical methods, because these have less impact on the balance of the tank ecosystem. For example, if you kill off all the algae at once with a chemical, this leads to a reduction in water quality, to the extent that the filter may not be able to cope effectively. Some fish and snails browse on algae, helping to keep it in check. Take out the tank decor and treat it separately, to reduce stress on the fish. Look for potential causes of the problem, too, so you can prevent a recurrence: Excess algae often results from too much light, high nitrate levels, and is more likely in a tank without plants.

If your plants are being eaten because the tank contains too many snails (see page 69), you may be tempted to kill the snails with a molluscicide. Even after using a treatment of this kind, you will still need to collect them up, otherwise the water quality will deteriorate rapidly as they decompose. A better course of action is to remove the snails by hand or to net them, and to destroy the snail eggs as they are laid to prevent future problems.

WATER QUALITY

Good water quality is vital for the fish's well-being, and poor conditions can cause real harm. Once the chlorine or chloramine has been removed, you must monitor the water quality regularly, especially in a new tank, to prevent a potentially fatal build-up of ammonia and nitrite. Even at relatively low levels, these chemicals may reduce the fish's resistance to disease, leaving them at greater risk from opportunist infections. Establishing a routine for monitoring water quality and partial water changes (see pages 80–81) will ensure that they do not suffer from any environmental disease.

Signs of illness

With most types of illness, fish exhibit visible signs that they are afflicted – such as physical symptoms or changes in their typical behaviour or movements. Keen observation of the fish is vital when it comes to recognizing these indicators. Are they swimming normally? Do they seem sluggish?

Study the fish closely every day when you feed them. Are they all eating well? Healthy fish are generally hungry, eating small amounts through the day, although they may not eat for a short period after a move. There are various reasons why a fish may not eat, but if unresolved, then the fish will become weaker over time and more likely to succumb to fungus. Also note if any fish spit out their food immediately. This can be an early sign of 'mouth fungus' (see page 101). With some species, it may be hard to tell how well they are eating, especially with catfish and other nocturnal feeders. Try feeding these fish last thing at night, with the aquarium lights off, to see if they show any interest in food.

Dropsy causes a fish's body to swell up, as shown here. There are numerous causes of this condition, some of which can be infectious, and treatment is generally very difficult.

Swimming

A fish is only likely to stop swimming in the terminal stages of an illness, when it will then simply float at the water's surface. You may notice some difficulty in swimming beforehand, however, depending to some extent on the nature of the illness. If the swim-bladder, which controls the fish's buoyancy, is affected, the fish will be unable to swim normally. You may see that it cannot dive effectively, tending to float to the surface.

With tropical fish, any sudden chilling of their environment can have this effect temporarily, so your first step should be to check the water temperature in the aquarium. If it seems that only one fish is affected, this may be simply a sign of old age, especially in the case of livebearers such as guppies (*Poecilia reticulata*).

A fish that repeatedly rubs itself against rocks and other decor in the aquarium is likely to be afflicted by some kind of irritation on its body. Poor water quality may affect the fish's behaviour in this way, or external parasites may be a possible cause (see pages 104–7).

Nutritional problems

Thanks to the development of well-balanced formulated foods, cases of nutritional diseases have now become very uncommon. Even so, do not use fish food past its recommended 'use by' date, or the fish could possibly start to suffer from a deficiency of certain key vitamins. This may cause them to swim in an unusual way, or

show other, more specific signs, such as haemorrhaging at the base of their fins. If you buy their food in cardboard tubs, make sure that these remain dry, because the food could turn mouldy if the base becomes at all damp. Fortunately, most brands of formulated fish food are now packed in waterproof plastic containers.

Setting up a hospital tank

While the idea of setting up a separate hospital tank may seem over-cautious, it may be very valuable, both in helping a sick fish recover, and in minimizing the possible spread of disease or infection within the tank. Since most infections spread rapidly through water, it is advisable to separate the patient to this quarantine tank as soon as possible.

For a hospital tank, the aquarium need not be very large, depending on the size of the fish, and it should be sparsely furnished, with a bare floor. There is little point in setting up an undergravel filter, partly because the filter bed will not have time to mature, and also because the majority of medications used to treat fish are likely to harm the bacteria in the filter bed. It is better to use a simple sponge filter instead. The use of carbon in a filter is also not generally recommended for a hospital tank, because it can inactivate certain remedies, and may itself be adversely affected as a filter medium by others.

Do include some basic decor in the tank, to give the fish a sense of security, using weighted plastic plants which can be easily disinfected and will not require lighting. Depending on which species of fish are in the tank, you may also want to include one or two retreats or refuges, such as a broken flowerpot.

Once you are sure that the fish has recovered, you may return it to the main aquarium, transferring it with extra care to minimize stress. Carefully strip down the hospital tank, and wash all the components with an aquarium disinfectant, so that it is ready to be used again if necessary in the future.

Precautionary measures

If you suspect that the fish may be affected by a fungal problem (see pages 102–3) as well as a bacterial (pages 100–101) or parasitic infection (pages 104–5) do not be tempted to use two remedies simultaneously, unless you are certain that it is safe to do so. If you combine medications, you could even inadvertently poison the fish instead of curing them. In their already weakened state, this extra strain may well make them succumb completely. If you suspect you might need to use a combination of commercial remedies, check either with the store or the manufacturer; alternatively, you could seek the advice of an experienced fish vet.

PROTECTING EGGS AND FRY

When using any kind of medication or treatment for fish, add it in strict accordance with the instructions on the pack. If you give more than the recommended dose, this is likely to be counterproductive or even harmful. In general, you should not add medication to a tank including any eggs or young fry, unless it is absolutely essential, because it may affect their development. Check the contents carefully because heavy metals including copper, which is a component of many remedies, can be especially harmful, resulting in a high percentage of fry with developmental abnormalities. It is better to treat any ailing adults in a separate tank.

Many commercial remedies used for fish ailments are dyes, such as methylene blue, which may well stain the sealant in the tank. This unwanted side-effect, in addition to the risk of inactivating the filter system (if charcoal or biological, killing off beneficial bacteria), means that it is usually unwise to add remedies to the water in the main aquarium. It may be better to strip down and refill the main tank instead, to try to eliminate any infection.

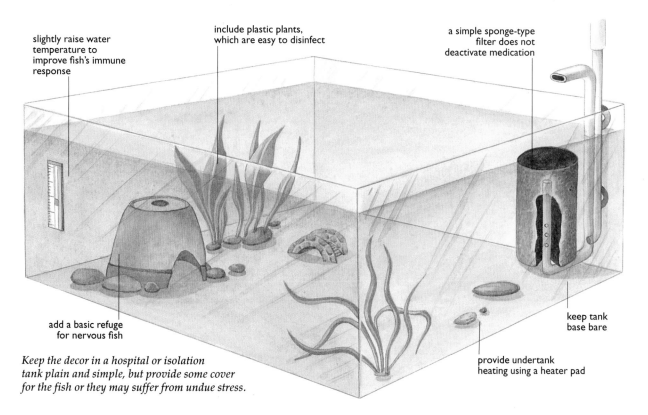

slightly raise water temperature to improve fish's immune response

include plastic plants, which are easy to disinfect

a simple sponge-type filter does not deactivate medication

add a basic refuge for nervous fish

keep tank base bare

provide undertank heating using a heater pad

Keep the decor in a hospital or isolation tank plain and simple, but provide some cover for the fish or they may suffer from undue stress.

Bacterial diseases

Although certain bacteria are clearly highly beneficial in the aquarium, helping to break down waste in a biological filtration system, others will be a serious threat to the health of the fish. Known as pathogenic bacteria, these are responsible for causing a range of infections and diseases. Fortunately, you can treat most of these problems successfully with antibiotics and similar anti-bacterial drugs.

The laws governing the supply and availability of antibiotics and other drugs of this type differ from country to country. In some places, they may only be available on veterinary prescription, such as in the UK, whereas in the US and some parts of continental Europe, you can buy remedies containing antibiotics over the counter from aquatic stores.

Methods of treatment

When administering medication, it is not just the power of the drug to overcome the bacteria that is significant. There is also the matter of how it is best applied for the greatest likelihood of success, which depends partly on the ailment and also on the type of fish and your set-up.

Medicinal bathing • The simplest method is to place the sick fish in an antibiotic bath. Do not add the drug to the main aquarium, because it will harm the beneficial bacterial population. This type of treatment can prove highly effective in overcoming external infections, such as in cases of fin rot for example (see right), although you will almost certainly have to repeat it on several occasions. It is unlikely to resolve more deep-seated infections.

Injections • In cases where there is an internal or more serious infection, it may be better to administer the antibiotic by injection. Clearly, this method is generally most suitable for large fish. It should be carried out by a veterinarian, preferably one who is experienced in dealing with piscine patients.

Minor fin damage can lead to a full-blown infection. If treated in the early stages, the damaged area may regrow.

Medicated food • A third method, incorporating the drug into the fish's food, is most often used commercially where a large number of fish require treatment – to combat an incidence of widespread infection, such as in a holding pond on a fish farm, for example. In some countries, you may be able to obtain small amounts of medicated fish food, suitable for use within the home aquarium. An obvious drawback of this method is that the fish can only benefit from the treatment if they are still eating, but with a number of bacterial illnesses, the fish typically lose their appetite.

Direct treatment

In some cases of bacterial infection, it can be helpful to apply the recommended treatment direct to the site of the infection. This approach is particularly useful when treating fish with some form of localized damage, such as an ulcer or fin rot (see right and picture, below). You can apply the medication quite easily using a cotton-wool bud or similar, delicate tool. Carefully lift the fish from the water with a suitable net, then quickly and gently dab the saturated material directly onto the site, ensuring that you treat the entire area, before lowering the fish back into the water. Never rub the affected area because this could worsen the state of the injury.

Care with carbon filters

One effective treatment used for the more common bacterial infections of fish is phenoxyethanol, which sometimes forms the basis of proprietary bacterial treatments in cases where antibiotic remedies are not available. You must never use this chemical in a tank with a canister filter that contains carbon. The toxic and waste substances that have been absorbed by the carbon during the filtration process are unfortunately liberated by phenoxyethanol, releasing them back into the water with calamitous results.

Fin rot

When fish suffer from an initial bacterial infection, the affected area may then be invaded by pathogenic fungi as well. Fin rot is a typical example. Fish with long fins are most susceptible, because their fins are most prone to damage; harmful microbes colonize the damaged areas, and so the infection spreads. Any injury to the fins, including fin-nipping by other fish, can lead to fin rot. Fish that are spawning may also be vulnerable, especially females that have been harassed by males.

Early treatment should resolve this particular disorder rapidly, and the affected rays will regenerate without problems. If neglected, however, the infection develops into an illness that affects the whole system and which will become life-threatening.

Piscine tuberculosis

This is undoubtedly the most serious bacterial disease a fish-keeper will encounter, partly because it may lead to numerous deaths in the aquarium, but also because it may be transmitted to people (see below). Unfortunately, the symptoms associated with piscine tuberculosis are fairly non-specific, and apply to various other diseases as well. This is a chronic disease,

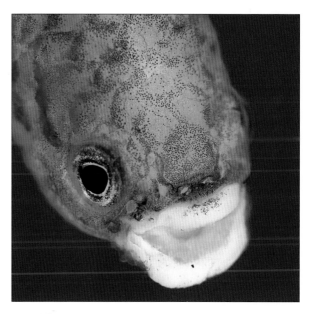

Mouth fungus can be life-threatening if the signs are not recognized early enough. Once the fish stops eating properly, its resistance to disease will soon fall drastically.

with fish losing their appetites and wasting away. There may be other symptoms, such as protruding eyes, known as exophthalmia or pop-eye (see page 107).

If several fish in the tank die, arrange a veterinary examination of the deceased fish. It will cost relatively little, and can be very valuable in saving the other fish, in cases where treatment is practical. If piscine tuberculosis is diagnosed, however, then euthanasia is recommended. After an outbreak of this disease, discard the substrate and plants, and wash the tank and other equipment with an iodophor disinfectant to eliminate the bacterium before restocking.

Mouth fungus

In spite of its name, mouth fungus, which is also known as 'cotton wool disease' is actually caused by *Flexibacter* bacteria. Outbreaks may usually be traced to poor water conditions or fish that have recently been introduced to the aquarium. In the early stages, affected fish may spit out their food, rather than swallowing it. Signs of the characteristic cotton wool growth are also apparent between their scales. At this stage, there is a good chance that the affected fish will recover if given appropriate treatment. Another symptom you may notice is shimmying, with affected fish moving slightly from side to side without actually swimming forwards.

Fungal and viral diseases

The average aquarium may contain a wide range of fungal spores in the water – no matter how clean it may look – and they are certainly present in the environment outside the tank. In many cases, these spores are not a problem and do not cause disease, although they may strike if the fish sustains even a minor injury – perhaps from combat with another fish, or rough handling when it was caught.

As with all health problems, prevention is better than cure. Poor environmental conditions can foster fungal growth. Decomposing food or dead plant leaves left in the water may well cause problems, so always maintain clean, well-oxygenated water and remove debris and uneaten food.

Viral problems, by contrast, are unlikely to occur unless you add a fish to the aquarium that is already infected. This is why it is wise to isolate new fish at first, to ensure that they are healthy and do not present a hazard to those already established in the tank.

Fungus may affect the whole body as well as the fins, as with this fire-mouthed cichlid, which is suffering from widespread body fungus. Damage to the scales often predisposes fish to fall victim to fungus, so early treatment is necessary.

FUNGAL DISEASES

One of the advantages of a new aquarium containing treated fresh water is that it should be relatively free from fungal contamination, so that the risk of fungal diseases is at least reduced in this context. As a precautionary measure, you should always treat the site of any obvious injury to help prevent fungal infection, which would delay healing. An unattended wound is more likely to result in an infection taking hold, often indicated by a haloed effect at first, before the fungus starts to resemble cotton wool. If one or both eyes are affected, they will take on a cloudy appearance.

Treating fungal infections

There are various commercial remedies available for treating fungal infections, as well as the traditional method – a solution of malachite green which is painted directly onto any fungus developing on the body. Net the fish carefully, laying it in the net on its side on a piece of paper towel that has been dipped in the aquarium water. Keep the net slightly raised to prevent the fish from leaping out, and so that the affected area is accessible. Treat the site of the infection directly, using a small paintbrush to apply the malachite green solution with gentle dabs. This can help the healing process significantly.

Fungal attacks on eggs

In some cases, fungus may also strike the fish's eggs, although fertilized eggs do seem to have some resistance to fungal attack. This problem is likely to be greatest in cases where a relatively high proportion of the eggs are infertile, although those of some species, such as bumblebee gobies (*Brachygobias xanthozona*), appear to be more susceptible to fungal infection than others.

As a precaution, you can help to safeguard the eggs by treating the water with a commercial anti-fungal product. It is preferable to try to minimize problems in the first place, however: make sure that the breeding tank or hatching tank you are using for the eggs only contains fresh, treated water. This should be relatively free from fungal spores, in comparison with water that has being drawn from the main aquarium where levels of contamination and fungal spores are likely to be higher.

VIRAL DISEASES

Fortunately, relatively few viruses are of great significance as far as tropical aquarium fish are concerned. For example, carp pox is far more common in coldwater cyprinids such as goldfish (*Carassius auratus*), compared with their tropical relatives. There are indications that the full extent of viral infections may have been underestimated, however, and research continues on the subject. A virus has now been implicated as the likely cause of Singapore angel disease (SAD), for example, an illness with a very high mortality rate that afflicts angelfish (*Pterophyllum* species) bred commercially in this region.

Unfortunately, viruses use the fish's own cell mechanisms to reproduce themselves. This makes it especially difficult to devise drugs to treat this kind of infection, simply because they are likely to disrupt normal body processes when attacking the virus – humans have the same problem in treating the common cold, which is viral in origin. Active prevention of viral disease is therefore still the favoured approach for trying to combat these illnesses at present, using vaccinations to protect susceptible fish. This also

This close-up view shows the signs of lymphocystis, one of the most widespread viral diseases of fish. Unfortunately, there is no treatment available, although the inclusion of vitamin C in the fish's diet may help to reduce the risk of infection.

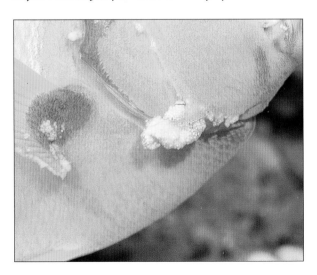

activates the fish's immune system, helping it to overcome any subsequent viral challenge. Quarantining new fish initially to make sure they are showing no signs of illness is the best way of preventing a potential widespread viral problem in the aquarium.

Lymphocystis

This condition is the most widespread form of viral disease encountered in tropical fish. It is possible that environmental factors, including pollution, may also affect the incidence of these tumours. An increase in the levels of heavy metals in the water has been linked with an above-average occurence of tumours in fish.

Lymphocystis causes swellings over the body surface and fins. These growths increase in size over time, often assuming a cauliflower-like appearance. Aside from disfiguring the fish, however, they do not generally cause any real harm, although this partly depends on their location on the body.

Fortunately, lymphocystis is not highly infectious, but if an infected individual comes into close contact with another fish that has an injury, there is a much greater likelihood that the disease will be transmitted. In any case, you should isolate any affected individuals to prevent the possible spread of infection. There is no effective treatment, although there have been claims that abrading the lesion may be successful; it is thought this may help to trigger the fish's immune response, enabling it to overcome the infection.

In a few cases, lymphocystis may also strike the internal body organs; the growth usually first becomes apparent by exerting pressure from within, interrupting the natural profile of the fish's body. In this instance, where the tumour may well affect how the internal organs function, euthanasia may be necessary.

Malawi bloat

This remains rather a mysterious illness, which is associated with cichlids originating from Lake Malawi and neighbouring East African lakes, as its name suggests. A virus has been suspected as the cause, but it is possible that other factors could be responsible as well. The symptoms resemble those of dropsy, with the fish developing a swollen body. The scales become lifted and raised away from the body, rather than forming a sleek body casing. Fish showing these signs should be set apart in an isolation tank. In some cases, there may also be other symptoms – pop-eye or exophthalmia (see page 107) is sometimes seen with this condition, and fluid may accumulate in the body cavity. In such cases, the prognosis is poor.

Parasitic infections

Tropical fish are unfortunately vulnerable to a number of parasites, which may seriously threaten their health. Some parasites are highly specific, tending to attack only particular groups of fish, while others may infect any species. Fish parasites may be broadly divided into two groups – external and internal: external parasites produce visible symptoms on the outside of the fish's body, whereas internal parasites may occur in the intestinal tract, for example. This type of problem usually results from the introduction of an infected individual to the aquarium, highlighting the value of isolating any new aquisitions in a separate tank before you add them to the main aquarium.

White spot

This is probably the most common of the various protozoal diseases. It is sometimes known as 'ich' because it is caused by a unicellular micro-organism called *Ichthyophthirius multifiliis*. An infection of this type can seriously damage the fish, with certain species such as black mollies (*Poecilia sphenops*) apparently being more susceptible than others.

The obvious symptom of the disease is the presence of the tiny white spots which appear all over the fish's body, but this is only one part of the parasite's life cycle.

A rasbora with the characteristic signs of white spot. This often debilitates the fish, making it more susceptible to fungus.

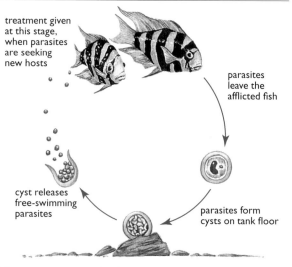

treatment given at this stage, when parasites are seeking new hosts

parasites leave the afflicted fish

parasites form cysts on tank floor

cyst releases free-swimming parasites

The parasite responsible for the common condition known as white spot spreads readily through the water, presenting a major health hazard to fish in the aquarium.

The spots then rupture, giving rise to tomites, which are the parasites at their free-living stage. Each spot can produce as many as 1000 tomites. In the wild, relatively few of these would be able to locate a suitable host, but within the confines of the aquarium, where the stocking density is often relatively high, all the occupants are then at serious risk of being attacked by the tomites.

These tomites must find a host almost immediately – typically within a day, depending on the water temperature – otherwise they will die. Once they come into contact with a fish, they embed themselves in its body, forming the trophozoite stage which ultimately gives rise to the characteristic white spots. The fish's body then becomes damaged by the parasites, and these areas are much more susceptible to attack by other microbes, especially types of opportunistic bacteria and fungi. Weakened by recurrent white spot infections, affected fish soon start to die, while treatment can only be effective against the tomite stage in the life cycle. Work is progressing on the development of a vaccine, but proprietary remedies should give good results if applied at the correct stage.

Unfortunately, it appears that some fish may carry this infection without showing clinical signs unless they are stressed, so you may not notice crucial warning signs. This explains why white spot sometimes crops up unexpectedly in an established community aquarium. Never use the same net between an aquarium where white spot is present and a healthy tank, because you will almost inevitably transfer some tomites in the droplets of water adhering to the net.

Velvet disease

This disease is caused by another protozoal parasite called *Oodinium*. Danios and labyrinth fish are among the most susceptible tropical species to velvet disease. Fish that have become infected often scrape themselves on rocks and other objects in the aquarium to ease the irritation caused by these parasites boring into their skin. If you look closely, you may notice that affected fish have a yellowish-grey hue on their bodies. There may also be some obvious yellow speckling, especially on the fins if these are normally clear, which is why this illness is also sometimes called 'gold dust disease'.

It is vital to remove any affected fish as soon as you spot any warning symptoms, and treat them without delay, partly to reduce the likely spread of infection. In some fish, you may notice their breathing has become more laboured than usual – a likely indication that the gills have been attacked by the parasites. At this point, the fish may die suddenly since their ability to extract oxygen from the water will be severely reduced.

Oodinium is an unusual microscopic organism, which is part animal and part plant. Like plants, it contains the green pigment chlorophyll so it can make its own food by photosynthesis, but it also hunts microbes. After attaching to the fish for up to a week, each parasite swells up and ruptures, releasing as many as 200 spores. In an aquarium, these spores have little difficulty in finding a host to infect, and so the cycle continues. They anchor themselves on the fish's body by developing a root-like structure.

It is a good idea to raise the water temperature slightly, because this increases the speed of the parasite's life cycle. As a result, the spores must find a host more quickly, or they will die in as little as just one day. Without this catalyst of increased temperature, they may survive for five days or even longer.

Neon tetra disease

In spite of its name, this illness also affects fish other than neon tetras (*Paracheirodon innesi*), although it is most commonly associated with this species. One of the most characteristic signs of the disease is a loss of coloration, usually a pale area that spreads over part of the body below the dorsal fin; in neon tetras themselves, the distinctive red stripe running down their sides becomes noticeably less vivid.

The infection results from a microsporidium parasite called *Pleistophora hyphessobryconis*, which cannot be treated with any great success at present. Even if any fish do survive, the likelihood is that they will retain the organism in their body and so continue to represent a hazard to other fish. In fact, this is how the infection is usually introduced to the aquarium. Fish that are apparently healthy may carry the infection, releasing the infective spores when under stress. Like those of similar parasites, the spores spread rapidly to other susceptible individuals in the aquarium.

Neon tetra disease is predominantly linked with its namesake fish, but can affect other species as well. This parasitic ailment often spreads rapidly, and cannot yet be treated effectively.

Other parasitic problems

While some of the major and most common parasitic illnesses are the result of infection by a single type of protozoan, others can be caused by a range of different organisms. Some of these microscopic parasites represent a major health hazard in the aquarium, and are difficult to eradicate.

Hole-in-the-head

This condition is associated with cichlids, especially discus (*Symphysodon aequifasciata*). It is the result of infection by a protozoan parasite called *Hexamita*, which is sometimes present in the digestive tract of this group of fish, where it normally causes no harm. If the fish are weakened by stress, however, the parasite multiplies and the fish's condition deteriorates.

Hole-in-the-head disease is a relatively common parasitic problem associated with discus. Look closely for the small, pale areas around the head, which then erupt and ulcerate.

One of the earliest signs of this disease are small pale areas visible on the head. Left untreated, these pale areas coalesce, causing erosion of the tissue, which also opens the way for secondary infection. Medicating the water with specific drugs of the metridazole group can overcome the infection before it develops into a life-threatening condition. Even if the fish recovers, scarring is likely, so rapid treatment is vital to minimize damage. Another sign is the presence of abnormal whitish faeces, which tend to hang behind the fish as it swims, indicating a disturbance to the digestive tract.

Outbreaks are commonly linked with stress, but adding vitamin C to the fish's diet (which is now routinely included in most formulated foods) should help to prevent outbreaks of hole-in-the-head, as will incorporating greenstuff in the form of some kind of vegetable matter. Research indicates that there may also be a link betwen water quality and this disease. Discus have highly specific needs in terms of water conditions, and, if these are not met, they may be more prone to attack from *Hexamita* parasites.

Slimy skin

This infection may involve a variety of different pathogens, and results from an increased output of mucus by the fish's body, in response to skin irritation. The fish's skin takes on a greyish-white colour, which tends to obscure the coloration beneath. A number of different protozoa can cause this problem, and secondary bacterial infections often also occur. It may usually be treated successfully, if caught at an early stage.

Other non-specific infections

A wide range of microbes including protozoa may also be implicated in cases of gill disease. This is relatively common in newly-acquired fish, which show obvious signs of discomfort when breathing, with rapid gill movements suggesting that they are having difficulty in drawing enough oxygen from the water. They will also be less active than normal, sometimes remaining inert for long periods.

Careful management is required to ensure the fish's recovery. Although poor environmental conditions almost certainly contributed to their condition in the first place, it is not a good idea to transfer the fish to dechlorinated fresh tap water, especially if a water conditioner is accidentally omitted. It is better to place them in an isolation tank containing equal amounts of aquarium water and treated tap water. Maintain the temperature at a slightly higher level than normal, because this helps to improve their immune response.

Pop-eye

In cases of exopthalmia, the eyes protrude abnormally, giving rise to its alternative name of pop-eye. The condition may result from quite a wide range of causes. It may be linked with eye flukes (see below) or a bacterial infection such as piscine tuberculosis (see page 101), and either one or both eyes may be affected. If there is just an isolated case, then the cause is more likely to be parasitic rather than bacterial. Poor water quality is sometimes implicated in severe outbreaks of pop-eye. In order to treat the condition effectively, it is important to know the cause.

Internal parasites

It is often very difficult to recognize the signs of internal parasites (the helminths group), because the symptoms are less obvious and distinctive than in conditions caused by external parasites. For example, if a fish is suffering with a severe intestinal build-up of parasitic worms, it may appear slightly swollen and show difficulty in swimming, but these symptoms are not enough to make a diagnosis, and they could be linked with other conditions such as dropsy (see page 98).

Fortunately, internal parasites are generally unlikely to become established in an aquarium, simply because they have complex life cycles which involve both other vertebrates and invertebrates. The fish is merely the intermediate host, meaning that the parasite does not mature in its body. This later stage in its life cycle normally occurs only in the wild when the infected fish is eaten by a bird such as a kingfisher or by a mammal.

The immature larval tapeworms develop in the intestinal tract of the bird, and start producing eggs which are released from the body in the bird's droppings. The eggs are consumed by crustaceans, so fish can become infected by eating these invertebrates. Within the regulated and restricted habitat of the aquarium, daphnia given as live food can represent a threat to the fish, acting as possible intermediate hosts for the parasites at this stage. Only daphnia cultured in an environment where birds could not foul the water can be regarded as safe (see pages 94–5).

If these helminths do gain access to the fish's body, they may then escape from the intestines into the body cavity and continue their development there. In other cases, the helminths remain within the fish's intestinal

Internal parasites such as flukes are quite rare in aquaria, but may sometimes occur. They are not usually dangerous because their complex life cycles make it hard for them to survive.

tract. They may occasionally be noticeable, looking like a fine strand of white ribbon trailing from the fish's anus. Symptoms of infection in this case are far less common, aside from a general loss of condition.

In some cases, treatment may be successful, although it will help greatly if the parasite can be correctly identified in the first instance. There are many potential types of parasitic worms that may occasionally afflict fish, but it is typically individuals caught from wild habitats that are at greatest risk, rather than the majority that are reared on fish farms.

Eye flukes

Flukes in general may be recognized by their flattened shape. As with parasitic worms, their life cycles tend to be complex – with the notable exception of the skin fluke (*Gyrodactylus*) – so they are not a common problem in aquarium surroundings, nor is there a great risk of cross-infection.

The basic route of infection is similar to that of internal parasites, but the eggs hatch into free-living larvae, which seek out and infect aquatic snails. After beginning their development, the larvae then leave the mollusc and attack fish, boring into their bodies.

In the case of eye flukes, they migrate to this area of the body, and in mild cases, they will cause cloudiness and opacity of the affected eye. A large accumulation of these parasites may result in the lens becoming ruptured, resulting in blindness. Treatment is virtually impossible in any event, but fortunately, these parasites are rare in aquarium fish.

Coping in a crisis

Even the most careful aquarist may suddenly be faced with a crisis. You can protect the fish to a degree by trying to anticipate possible problems and by knowing how to respond appropriately and promptly if something goes wrong. Sensible precautions might including having a spare heaterstat available, in case the one in the tank fails when it is impossible to obtain a replacement quickly.

Poisons

Certain household chemicals that might seem inoffensive can actually prove deadly if they are drawn into the aquarium through the air pump. Aerosol products, such as those used to kill fleas on dogs and cats are especially dangerous for this reason, as are other insecticidal sprays, such as fly and bug killers. Try to avoid using such products in the home, certainly in the same room as the fish.

The specific signs will vary depending upon the chemicals concerned, but a sudden wipe-out of an apparently healthy aquarium of fish would strongly suggest poisoning as the cause of death. If you do discover dead and dying fish in the aquarium, you should obviously remove any fish that are still alive to a container of dechlorinated water immediately, in the hope that they will recover.

Tracing the source of the poison can prove to be difficult in some cases, but you should be suspicious of the water itself if symptoms develop soon after a partial water change. Perhaps you have forgotten to add the water conditioner, leaving the fish exposed to a potentially high level of chlorine or chloramine. Adding this without delay may well resolve the situation before there are any further fatalities.

Pesticides in tap water

Another possibility, if you notice signs of poisoning after a water change, is that the problem stems from pesticides in the tap water. Pyrethrins, or their artificial counterparts which are known as permethrins, are typically added to water to flush the pipework and kill off any invertebrates that might be present. Some species of fish are considerably more susceptible than others to these pesticides. When water companies are planning to add these chemicals, they normally advise local fish-keeping groups of their intentions, but you may prefer to contact your local water supplier directly to ascertain the situation.

WHAT TO DO IN A POWER FAILURE

When a power failure occurs, not only will the water temperature start to fall, but aeration will cease, compromizing the efficiency of a biological filter containing aerobic bacteria, and the lights will go off. The most serious long-term effects may be on the filter, but there is little you can do to safeguard its efficiency.

Insulate the tank • The first action you must take is to insulate the aquarium by covering it, and so minimize heat loss from the water. Use a thick blanket or even a duvet or quilt for this purpose.

Monitor the temperature • You can keep a check on the temperature without having to open the hood. Provided that the room itself is reasonably warm, then the temperature should only decline slowly, enabling the fish to adjust gradually with no major ill-effects if the power supply is restored without too much delay.

Prevent fire hazards • Never cover the air pump, or leave the lights switched on, because the restoration of power may cause the covering to catch alight, if it occurs unexpectedly at night while you are asleep.

Extended power loss

It is not a good idea to add hot water to the aquarium, even if you have an alternative source of power that enables you to heat water. The fluctuating temperatures will be more stressful for the fish, and boiling also affects the relative hardness of the water, altering the water chemistry within the aquarium. In any event, you could not add any warmer water without removing some of the existing water, and if you needed to repeat the procedure to maintain the temperature, you would exceed the recommended volume change. Floating a hot water bottle on the surface, or placing one or two around the outside, is a much safer option to provide additional warmth if the power is off for a long period.

WARNING

In some cases, signs of poisoning may not be immediately obvious. You should not allow smoking in the same room as the tank; studies have shown that tobacco smoke absorbed into the water can cause subsequent malformation of the fry of pregnant guppies (*Poecilia reticulata*) and may even result in the death of adult fish.

blanket draped over the tank keeps in warmth

avoid lifting the tank lid and letting out warm air

use hot water bottle in prolonged power failures

Tropical fish can generally adapt quite well to a gradual drop in the temperature of their water during a power failure, but try to minimize the problem by insulating the tank.

What to do afterwards

The lack of illumination will do no harm in the short term, but once the power is restored, it is a good idea to leave the lights on for the usual amount of time. The heaterstat will then switch on again, and the water will warm up slowly, so that, as before, the fish should not be unduly stressed by the changing water temperature.

Check the filter • Check that the filter is working properly after being switched off; if the power has been off for long, you may want to add a beneficial culture of bacteria to seed the filter bed again.

Monitor water quality • Keep a close watch on the levels of ammonia and nitrite in the water after a power failure, to check that the bacterial population has not been badly damaged by the shortage of oxygen. If necessary, you will have to use zeolite sachets and activated carbon to remedy the damage in the short term until you are sure that the biological capacity of the filter is fully restored.

Observe the fish • The fish should recover without problems, with the water temperature rising gradually once the heater is switched on again. Watch them closely for the first week or so afterwards, however, for signs of an opportunistic fungal or bacterial infection as the result of being chilled.

Coping with a dying fish

If you ever find a fish beyond hope of recovery, it should be killed humanely and quickly to prevent further suffering. A vet can do this for you, but you may prefer not to subject your fish to the additional stress of being caught and transported to the surgery. If the fish is small, crushing it quickly with a block is probably the most humane method, but with a larger individual, cutting through the spinal cord behind the neck and decapitating it is a better option.

Never flush a dying fish down the toilet or drain. This is cruel, and could prolong its suffering considerably. Nor should sickly small fish ever be offered to larger carnivorous species, since this can spread the infection through your collection, as well as possibly giving the sick fish a protracted end. If you are unsure as to the cause of death of a number of fish, keep the bodies cool and take them for autopsy to your local veterinary surgery as soon as possible after death, along with a sample of the aquarium water plus details of their care.

Index

A

acidity 57
aggression 18–9, 26–7, 84
air pump 65
airlines 65
algae 82, 96
alkalinity 56
ammonia 49, 80
anabantoids 34–5
anatomy 10–1, 90
aquariums 44–5, 72–5,
cleaning 82–3
lighting 66–7
setting up 62–5
siting 60–1
aquatic plants 26, 48–51, 65,
  67, 71
archer fish 70
autopsies 109

B

bacteria 83, 96, 100-1
barbels 13, 75
behaviour 16–7, 18–9, 20–1, 75
blind cave fish 12, 33
bloodworms 95
body shape 16–7
bogwood 63
brackish water 14, 59, 70–1
breathing 10
breeding 18, 20–1, 26–7, 84–5
brine shrimps 89
bubble nests 21, 87
buoyancy 11, 98
buying fish 72–3
butterfly fish 42

C

carbon filters 52–3, 101
carnivores 90–1
catching fish 78–9
catfish 40–1, 91
catfish pellets 92–3
characins 32–3
chemicals 97

chlorine poisoning 68
choosing fish 26–7, 31, 72–5
cichlid sticks 92–3
cichlids 38–9
circulatory system 15
colour 75, 84
commercial breeders 24–5
community aquariums 18, 26–7,
conditioners 68–9
cotton wool disease 101
crickets 95
cyprinids 30–1

D

daphnia 88, 94
development 8–9, 22–3,
digestive system 90
digital thermometers 76–7
dropsy 98
dyes 47, 99

E

earthworms 95
egg-layers 20–1, 87
electrical impulses 13
evolution 8–9
exhibitions 73
eye flukes 107

F

feeding 75, 85, 88–9, 90–5
fertilizers 82
fibre 93
filling tanks 64
filter wool 83
filtration 52–3, 57, 62, 65, 77, 83, 86
fin rot 101
fins 17, 75, 101
fish-feeders 91
fish-keeping 24–5
fish stockists 25, 72–3
floating food 93
flowerpots 63
flukes 107
fluorescent tubes 66–7

foam cartridge filters 53
freshwater species 14, 59
frogs 68
fruit-flies 95
fry 22–3, 88–9
fungal infections 102–3

G

gills 10, 106
glassfish 70
gravel 46–7, 62
gravel cleaners 81

H

handling fish 68
health care 96–109
hearing 12
heaters 54–5
herbivores 91
hole-in-the-head disease 106
hoods 66–7
hospital tank 98–9
hydra 94, 96
hydrometer 71

I

illness 96–7
infection 75, 106–7
injections 100
infusoria culture 89
introducing new fish 19, 76–7
ion exchange resin 59
isolation tank 76, 96, 98–9

K

killifish 36–7

L

lateral line 13
leaf fish 43
lights and lighting 60, 66–7, 86
live food 94–5
livebearers 20–1, 28–9, 87

loaches 43
lungfish 10–1
lymphocystis 103

M

mail order 73
Malawi bloat 103
marbles 87
marine species 14, 59
mating 17
media filters 53
medicinal bathing 100
mesh 87
minerals 92–3
mouth fungus 101
mutations 23

N

neon tetra disease 105
nets 79
new tank syndrome 77
nitrate 49, 80
nitrite 49, 80
nitrogen cycle 49
nutrition 92–3, 98

O

osmosis 14

P

pair-bonding 21
parasites 104–7
parent fish 22–3
peat bases 47
pesticdes 108
pH 56–9
photosynthesis 48, 66
piscine tuberculosis 101
planting 50–1, 65, 67, 82–3, 87, 97
poisoning 68, 108
pop-eye 107
power supply 61, 66–7, 79, 81, 108–8
precautionary measures 99
predators 91
protecting eggs 87, 99, 102
proteins 92–3

R

rearing 88–9
rearing foods 88–9
rinsing gravel 47, 81

S

safety 61, 66–7, 81, 97, 108–9
salinity 71
sand 47
scales 9, 75
scats 71
scientific names 27
sealants 45
second-hand tanks 45, 62
senses 12–3
settling in 76–7
sexing 85
showing fish 27, 73
sight 12
Singapore angel disease 103
sinking wafers 93
siphoning 81
siting fish 60–1
slimy skin 106
snails 68, 97
sociability 18–9, 27
spawning 84–5, 87
special diets 93
spiny fish 79
starter kits 45
stress 97
substrate 46–7
suckermouth catfish 42, 91
swim bladder 11, 98
swimming 98

T

tails 17
tank decor 62–3, 86, 97
tanks 31, 44–5, 60–3, 64–7, 82–3, 86, 98–9
taste 13
temperature 14–5, 77, 85
territories 19, 26–7, 45
testing water 56–7
thermostats 54–5
tobacco smoke 108
trace elements 59, 82–3

traffic light system 18–9
transporting fish 25, 73, 76
treating fish 100–1
trickle filters 52
tubifex worms 95

U

undergravel filtration 52, 86

V

velvet disease 105
viral diseases 103
vitamins 92–3
volume 44

W

water conditions 14, 56–9, 68–9, 70–1, 80–1, 85, 97, 108–9
water hardness 58–9
water softeners 59
white spot 104
whiteworms 95

Z

zeolite 53, 57, 109

AUTHOR'S ACKNOWLEDGEMENTS
The author would like to thank Rita Hemsley for her help in typing up the manuscript for this book.

PUBLISHER'S ACKNOWLEDGEMENTS
Mitchell Beazley would like to thank the following organizations and people for their help in producing this book:

PAGEOne, (book packagers) Cairn House, Elgiva Lane, Chesham, Buckinghamshire HP5 2JD

Illustrations Karen Cochrane 44, 52, 60; Anthony Duke 8, 14, 15, 56, 92, 104 above; Liz Gray 9, 10, 11, 13, 14, 17, 48 above, 66 above, 86, 90, 99, 104 above

Photography Tim Ridley 46, 47, 48, 49, 50, 51, 53, 54, 55, 57, 61, 63, 64, 65, 66 below, 68, 71 below, 76, 77, 78, 79, 80, 81, 82, 83, 89 above, 91 below, 93, 94, 95, 108

Symbols Mark Bracey, Karen Cochrane.

Tanks and equipment supplied by Rolf C. Hagen (UK) Ltd., California Drive, Whitwood Industrial Estate, Castleford, West Yorkshire, WF10 5QH

PICTURE CREDITS
1 Photomax; 2 Photomax; 7 Oxford Scientific Films / Max Gibbs; 9 Photomax; 10 Photomax; 11 NHPA / Daniel Heuclin; 12 Photomax; 13 Photomax; 14 Photomax; 16 Photomax; 18 Photomax; 19 Photomax; 20 Photomax; 21 Photomax; 22 Photomax; 23 Photomax; 24 BBC Natural History Unit; 25 NHPA / Photomax; 26 Photomax; 27 Photomax; 28 Photomax; 29 Photomax; 30 Photomax; 31 Photomax; 32 Photomax; 33 Photomax; 34 Photomax; 35 Photomax; 36 above NHPA / Gerard Lacz; 36 below Oxford Scientific Films / Max Gibbs; 38 Photomax; 39 above Photomax; 39 below Oxford Scientific Films / Max Gibbs; 39 below left Photomax; 40 Photomax; 41 Photomax; 42 Photomax; 43 Photomax; 58 NHPA; 67 Photomax; 69 left Photomax; 69 right Oxford Scientific Films / G I Bernard; 70 Photomax; 71 above Photomax; 72 Photomax; 73 Photomax; 74 Oxford Scientific Films / Max Gibbs; 84 NHPA; 85 Oxford Scientific Films / Max Gibbs; 87 Photomax; 88 Photomax; 89 below Oxford Scientific Films / Max Gibbs; 91 above Photomax; 96 Oxford Scientific Films / Max Gibbs; 97 Oxford Scientific Films / Max Gibbs; 98 Photomax; 100 Photomax; 101 Photomax; 102 Photomax; 103 Photomax; 104 below Photomax; 105 Photomax; 106 Photomax; 107 Oxford Scientific Films / Max Gibbs; Front cover Photomax; Back jacket both Photomax